MOSTLY DOWNHILL IN THE PEAK DISTRICT:

The White Peak

Clive Price

SIGMA Leisure

Copyright © Clive Price, 1994

Published by Sigma Leisure - an imprint of
Sigma Press, 1 South Oak Lane, Wilmslow, Cheshire SK9 6AR, England.

British Library Cataloguing in Publication Data
A CIP record for this book is available from the British Library.

ISBN: 1-85058-384-6

Typesetting and Design by: Sigma Press, Wilmslow, Cheshire.

Cover design: The Agency

Cover photograph: The author in Monsal Dale (Chris Rushton)

Printed by: J.W. Arrowsmith Ltd, Bristol

Preface

I hope that this volume of walks will encourage families with very young children and people who do not want to struggle up long steep climbs to enjoy the beautiful scenery which the White Peak has to offer. By starting high and finishing low it is still possible to obtain the views that make this area so special.

Some years ago, when I was working for the BBC, I travelled to the Lake District to interview National Park Ranger, Malcolm Guyatt, about a special trail he was devising for people confined to wheelchairs. Malcolm, a mountaineer of no mean experience, said: "It's very easy for the likes of you and me to believe that the best views of the mountains can be obtained only from above. In fact, the views from the valley floor looking upwards are often far better."

That is as true of the Peak District as it is of the Lakes.

One advantage of these short walks is that they allow sufficient time for the walker to pause frequently in order the admire the scenery or to examine a building or other point of interest. They are not intended for the mile gobbler but for those who wish to explore the countryside at leisure and to savour everything which it has to offer.

The word 'downhill' needs defining. Quite briefly it means that the walk starts at a higher altitude than the one at which it finishes. In many cases the topography will dictate minor climbs in between but these have been kept to a minimum. Sometimes the rate of descent will be steep, at others gradual or even imperceptible. Occasionally the routes are little more than pleasant strolls.

Using Public Transport

I have tried to select starting and finishing points accessible by public transport, whether it be by train or bus. In the northern section of the White Peak I have taken advantage of the Hope Valley railway line which links

Manchester with Sheffield and serves numerous intermediate stations. Fortunately the White Peak is also blessed with several long-distance bus routes such as the R1 'Transpeak', whick links Manchester with Buxton, Bakewell, Matlock, Derby and Nottingham, and the X23 from Hanley through Leek, Buxton and Bakewell to Sheffield. The X65 operates between Sheffield and Buxton while the X66 joins Chesterfield with Buxton. Another regular daily service is the X67 from Chesterfield to Manchester.

These are obviously the arterial routes but other services from towns such as Bakewell, Buxton and Matlock make outlying villages accessible by public transport. Some services run on market days and Saturdays, mainly for the benefit of local inhabitants, but there is always room and a welcome for the rambler.

Thanks to the National Park there are several subsidised services which operate on summer Sundays and Bank Holidays, providing through routes from the urban centres outside the National Park. Sadly there are still some villages without any form of public transport. For these it will be essential to use a car, and for this reason I have also included details of parking.

In a book of this kind it is impossible to give the times of buses and trains but twice yearly, in May and November, Derbyshire County Council publishes a timetable for bus and train services at a cost of 50 pence. This is available at bus stations, National Park Information Centres and Tourist Information Centres. This timetable is backed up by a 'Busline' telephone service which is normally operational beween 7am and 8pm on the following numbers:

Derby (0332) 292200
Buxton (0298) 23098
Chesterfield (0246) 250450
Chester (0244) 402666
Wilmslow (0625) 534850
Stafford (0785) 223344

For train enquiries ring:

Manchester (061) 832 8353
Derby (0332) 332051

For those walking with children, or without someone to act as chauffeur at the end of the walk, the most feasible way of doing one of these walks will be to leave the car at the start, returning to it by public transport from the end of the walk; or by doing the reverse. The starting and finishing points are linked by public transport on the following walks:

Walk 1   Several buses between Castleton and Mam Nick, on summer Sundays only.

Walk 2   As for Walk 1.

Walk 3   Frequent daily service from Bamford to Castleton.

Walk 5   Bus from Chesterfield to Manchester runs from Stoney Middleton to Foolow twice daily.

Walk 6   As for Walk 5. Also linked by several buses daily on the Bakewell–Tideswell service.

Walk 10   Several buses daily between Baslow and Bakewell.

Walk 13   Several buses daily on the Bakewell–Tideswell service.

Walk 24   Buses from Ashbourne to Tissington on Thursdays, Saturdays, summer Sundays and Bank Holidays.

The following walks are possible on almost any day of the week by travelling to the start by one service and returning by another:

From Bakewell

Walk 11   Daily services both out to Birchover and back from Youlgreave.

Walk 12   Several buses out to Over Haddon on Tideswell service, and back from Alport on the Manchester–Nottingham service (daily, every 2 hours).

From Buxton

Walk 15   Daily service (except Sundays) out to Sheldon, returning from Ashford via Nottingham–Manchester service.

Walk 16   Daily service out to Monyash, returning from White Lodge via Nottingham–Manchester service.

Walk 17   Daily service out to Chelmorton; return from Wyedale via Nottingham–Manchester service.

Walk 18   Out to Taddington on Manchester–Nottingham service; return from Miller's Dale on the Chesterfield–Buxton or Sheffield–Buxton service.

All the remaining routes require the use of a car.

Planning Your Walk

All these walks have been researched on foot and follow public rights of way or concessionary footpaths. Nevertheless, the terrain can be rocky or muddy, so good, sound footwear should be worn at all times. Even on short, easy walks, accidents can happen – in the form of cuts on barbed wire or twisted ankles. Ensure that you always carry a small first-aid kit.

In our fickle climate the weather is liable to sudden change which makes it advisable to have rain gear and warm clothing in your rucksack.

The times suggested for each walk are meant only as a general guide: some will complete the walk more quickly, while others may exceed the time given. You will need to allow extra time if some of the attractions along the route are to be visited, and allow up to double the time given if walking with very young children.

Parents will be aware of their own children's capabilities and will, therefore, be the best judges of the suitability of each walk with regard to time and distance. However, some of the walks in this collection are better suited than others for very young children, for whom the difficulties of terrain make the following walks unsuitable:

Walk 1	There is one stretch of narrow path along a steep hillside.
Walk 7	This includes a long stretch along a very rocky path through woodlands, where there is a chance of a youngster spraining an ankle.
Walk 17	The middle section of this route involves a very rocky uneven path.
Walk 18	There is a steep descent alongside a quarry (although there is a barrier fence).

For the farmer the countryside is a workplace. Follow the country code and, in particular carry all your rubbish away with you and close all gates behind you. Stray cattle and sheep can prove a nightmare to the farmer, and sometimes result in severe financial loss. At all times, but especially during the lambing season, keep all dogs on a lead. During the grouse shooting season (12 August–31 December) certain areas of open access land on the high moors may be closed, but this does not affect public rights of way, which are open at all times.

I have listed places of refreshment, be they cafés, hotels or pubs. I have refrained from stating opening times because these do vary considerably. Most of the pubs mentioned provide bar meals both at lunchtime and in the evening but not always for the full duration of opening times. Some cafés are open all day every day of the year (except Christmas), while others close their doors during the winter and, in some cases, midweek during high season.

Several of these walks start from or finish at the same points. For that I make no apology. Two walks from the top of a hill can be so different in character; and as I said earlier many of the walks have been chosen to integrate with public transport.

Enjoy them ... as I did.

Acknowledgements

It is only fitting that I should thank all the people without whose help this volume would not have been possible. Graham Beech mentioned the idea and, after I had done the walking and the writing, saw it through all the production stages. Frank McGowan proved an invaluable chauffeur, even sacrificing some of his own precious walking time to rendezvous with me at the end of the walk. My granddaughter, Tamsin, accompanied me on several of the walks, so heightening my enjoyment of them.

Roland Smith, Head of Information at the Peak District National Park, was only too willing to supply information on a number of points. As in the companion volume, which covers the Dark Peak, I must mention the friendly bus drivers who ferried me to the starting points or from the finishing points. Last, but by no means least, thanks to my wife and daughters for their encouragement.

Clive Price

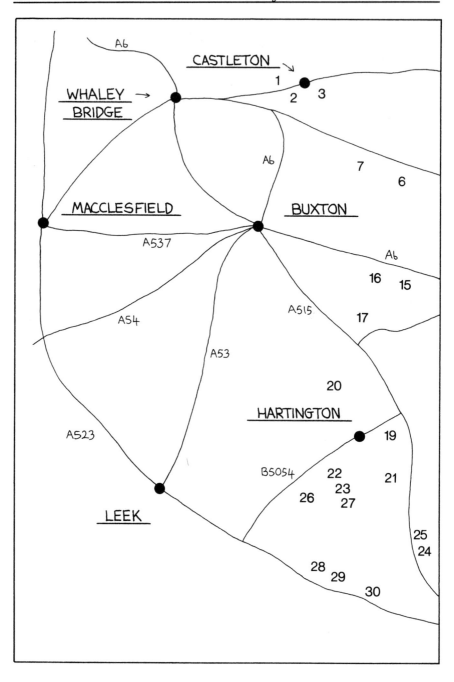

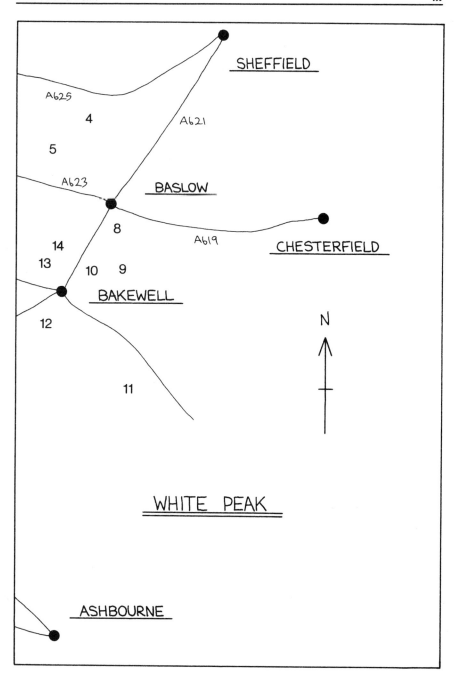

Contents

1. Cave Link

This walk, completely on field paths, links all the show caves of Castleton while passing beneath Peveril Castle.

Route: Mam Nick – Blue John Cave – Treak Cliff Cavern – Speedwell Cavern – Peak Cavern – Castleton.

Start: Car park, Mam Nick. Map reference 124833. Altitude 425 metres.

Finish: Car park, Castleton village. Map reference 149830. Altitude 197 metres.

Distance: 2¼ miles.

Duration: 1½ hours (allow extra if visiting caves).

Map: The Peak District: Dark Peak Area, number 1 in the Ordnance Survey Outdoor Leisure series.

Public Transport: Mam Nick has buses from Chesterfield on summer Sundays and Bank Holidays and from Macclesfield on a limited number of summer Sundays. On Saturdays a bus from Hanley, Leek and Buxton stops at the top of Winnats Pass which is about five minutes' walk from Mam Nick car park.

Castleton has daily buses from Sheffield and Chesterfield. On summer Sundays and Bank Holidays there are buses from Rochdale, Oldham, Ashton, Bakewell, Buxton, Barnsley, Mansfield, Ashbourne, Derby, Glossop and Manchester. There is a bus from Macclesfield on a limited number of summer Sundays and a bus from Hanley, Leek and Buxton on Saturdays. It may also be reached by train from Manchester and Sheffield, by catching a bus from Hope station.

By Car: The car parks at both Mam Nick and Castleton are signed from the A625 Chapel-en-le-Frith–Sheffield road. Cars may use the Winnats Pass.

Refreshments: There are cafés at some of the caves *en route*. In Castleton there is a choice of cafés and pubs serving bar meals both at lunchtime and in the evening.

Along the Way

The Caverns

The first of the show caves passed along our walk is the **Blue John Cavern** which was discovered some 300 years ago by miners. There are 14 veins of Blue John stone, eight of which have been mined for centuries. Next comes **Treak Cliff Cavern,** noted for the 'Pillar' – the largest piece of Blue John ever found. It also boasts a Dream Cave, a Fairyland Grotto and a Fossil Cave. Situated at the foot of the Winnats Pass is the **Speedwell Cavern** which is visited by boat along an old mine tunnel terminating at the top of the 'Bottomless Pit'. **Peak Cavern,** almost in the centre of Castleton village, has the largest cave entrance in Britain. It has the remains of a village where ropemakers once lived and the rope walk with the associated ropemaking machinery.

Peveril Castle

Constructed by William Peverel during the reign of William the Conqueror, this castle was intended to subdue and keep in check the troublesome local tribes of the area. It also served to protect the Crown's interests in the lead-mining industry. The most notable event in its history was the submission of King Malcolm IV of Scotland to King Henry II in 1157. In later reigns it was extended and refortified but eventually fell into a state of partial decay, the local farmers sometimes using it as a pinfold. In 1932 it passed into the ownership of the Ministry of Works, and is now managed by English Heritage.

Castleton

The village is one of the honeypots of the National Park. During Norman times the houses were laid out on a grid system and surrounded by a defensive ditch, parts of which may still be seen near the car park.

On 29 May every year the Castleton Garland ceremony is celebrated. This is not a special attraction laid on for the benefit of tourists although large numbers of visitors do attend. It may be a survival from pagan times, descended from fertility rites, but many experts believe it to have originated with the restoration of Charles II to the throne in 1660 following the Commonwealth period, during which festivities of any kind were frowned upon. A dome-shaped wooden frame, covered in greenery and topped with a smaller crown of fresh flowers known as 'The Queen', is worn by 'The King' as he rides round the village on horseback dressed in Stuart costume. He is accompanied by his 'Lady' and schoolgirls dressed in white. Music is provided by the village band, the main tune being but one note different from the Helston Floral Dance. In view of the migrations of Cornish miners to Derbyshire this is not surprising.

At the end of the procession the 'Queen' is removed from the garland and hoisted onto the church tower, a signal for the inhabitants to commence dancing through the streets.

Castleton from Peveril

Mam Tor

Our walk starts from the car park at Mam Nick which is a narrow defile between Rushop Edge and Mam Tor, called the 'Shivering Mountain' because parts of its eastern flank have experienced an enormous landslip. Its summit, a popular viewpoint, was once crowned with a prehistoric fort, and parts of the fort's outline may still be traced.

The Route

Exit from the lower section of the car park by turning left along the A625 for 200 yards. Turn right over a stile by a National Trust sign for Windy Knoll, a small area of land adopted as part of the Countryside Commission's Countryside Stewardship programme. Under the scheme, the owner is given extra cash in return for allowing increased public access and accepting an agreed management regime.

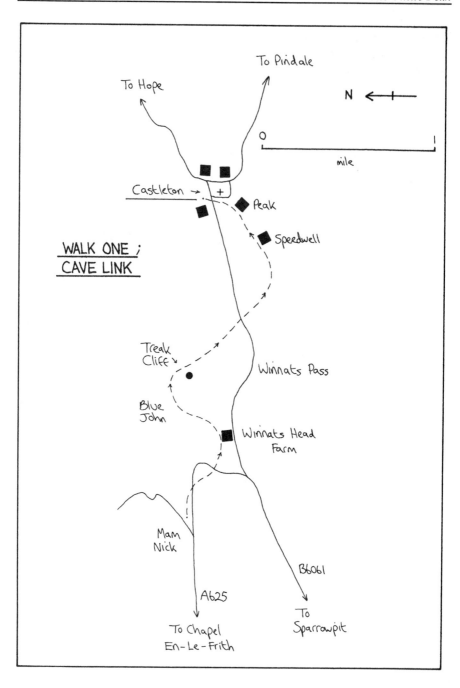

After approximately 20 yards, and with the small abandoned Windy Knoll quarry a short distance in front, fork left along a very green path – do not advance as far as the quarry where there is another path going off to the left. At this stage the shattered face of Mam Tor towers above to your left while Winnats Head Farm lies directly ahead. In the far distance it is possible, on a clear day, to pinpoint Back Tor and Win Hill.

On gaining a stile, cross a minor road to a second stile and maintain your line of direction, indicated by a yellow waymarker sign on a low wooden post. A National Trust sign indicates that this is Winnats Head Farm. Cross the grass pasture to a stile. Stay to the left of a wall surrounding a sheepfold with the farmhouse just beyond it.

Go forward a further 100 yards to a three-armed footpath finger post. Turn left, taking the path signposted to Blue John Cavern. This crosses a large field, to the right of a very shallow valley, to another waymarker post from where it commences to lose height as it curves right towards a conspicuous stile.

Pass to the left of the main buildings of the Blue John Cavern to a ladder stile beside a five-barred gate. Maintain direction, aiming for the left-hand side of a small grass slope, then swing slightly to the left to a further waymark, and cross the stile a few yards beyond it.

Follow the distinct but narrow path diagonally down the hillside. After 150 yards it veers round to the right. Some care is needed because there is a very steep slope on your left. Castleton village comes into view down in the valley ahead. The path, occasionally very stony, continues to lose height to a stile. Walk behind the buildings of Treak Cliff Cavern. At the far corner turn left down a short flight of steps to the café, then right down a second flight of steps to a concrete footpath.

After a further 100 yards, and by a second bench (just in case you are exhausted), fork right onto a narrow path leading to the end of a wall. Pass a little to the right of the wall; by a solitary hawthorn, the path then veers right along the lower slope of a hill until meeting a stile. Turn left, and remaining to the right of the wall, descend the rocky path to meet the road through the Winnats Pass.

Turn left, passing the Speedwell Cavern on your right. 300 yards beyond, make a right turn over a stone stile alongside a five-barred gate. Another National Trust sign informs you that this area is known as Longcliff. Follow the wide path with a wall to your immediate left. After some distance you move away from the wall and there are two stone barns down below, also to the left, before the wall returns to flank the path.

Go through a gated stile by a small metal gate. Some 200 yards beyond, where the wall corners, there is a Y-junction. Fork left, remaining alongside the wall and enjoying the gradual descent.

After the next metal gate the path becomes a walled lane until, by Dales House, it acquires a tarmac surface and a name, Goosehill. Cross Peakshole Water by a fine stone bridge, pausing long enough to admire the raucous mallard that frequent this delightful spot. To the right is a sign to Peak Cavern.

By Carlton Emporium fork left to partner the river until emerging onto the A625 by Three Roofs café. The car park is opposite.

2. Cave Dale

Although having the same starting and finishing points as Walk 1, this follows a completely different route along bridleways and paths while permitting us to appreciate the virtual impregnability of Peveril Castle.

Route: Mam Nick – Rowter Farm – Cave Dale – Castleton.

Start: Car park, Mam Nick. Map reference 124833. Altitude 425 metres.

Finish: Car park, Castleton village. Map reference 149830. Altitude 197 metres.

Distance: 3½ miles.

Duration: 2 hours.

Map: The Peak District: Dark Peak Area, number 1 in the Ordnance Survey Outdoor Leisure series.

Public Transport: Mam Nick has buses from Chesterfield on summer Sundays and Bank Holidays and from Macclesfield on a limited number of summer Sundays. On Saturdays there is a bus from Hanley, Leek and Buxton which stops at the top of the Winnats Pass, some five minutes' walk from the start.

Castleton has a daily bus service from Sheffield and Chesterfield. On summer Sundays and Bank Holidays there are buses from Rochdale, Oldham, Ashton, Bakewell, Buxton, Barnsley, Mansfield, Ashbourne, Derby, Glossop and Manchester. There is a bus from Macclesfield on a limited number of summer Sundays and a bus from Hanley, Leek and Buxton on Saturdays. It is also possible to reach Castleton from Sheffield and Manchester by train, catching a bus from Hope station.

By Car: The car parks at both Mam Nick and Castleton are signed from the A625 Chapel-en-le-Frith–Sheffield road. Cars may use the Winnats Pass.

Refreshments: There is a selection of pubs and cafés in Castleton.

Along the Way

Winnats Pass

Now macadamised, the route through this celebrated and impressive defile was formerly a packhorse route, and was part of the saltway from Cheshire to Sheffield. In 1758 it was incorporated into the turnpike road linking Sheffield and Manchester but was used less frequently after the construction of an alternative turnpike road from Castleton up the unstable flank of Mam Tor. (This road has been closed in recent years because of further landslips and the Winnats is back in use for cars and other light traffic.)

In 1758 a young couple eloping to Peak Forest, then the Gretna Green of the Peak District, were ambushed, robbed and murdered while travelling through the Winnats. Their bodies were buried in the Speedwell Cavern. The three miners known to have been responsible were never brought to justice but each died a terrible death.

Main Street, Castleton

Castelton

See Walk 1.

Peveril Castle

See Walk 1.

The Route

From the car park turn left along the A625 for 200 yards. Turn right over a stile by a National Trust sign for Windy Knoll, now a participant in the Countryside Commission's Countryside Stewardship programme.

After a further 200 yards, and with Windy Knoll's abandoned quarry a short distance ahead, fork right along a grassy path which, after rounding Windy Knoll itself, reaches a wall stile and the B6061. Turn right for 10 yards and then left through a gateway onto a bridleway. Mam Tor is behind you, Rushop Edge to your right.

With a stone wall on your left, follow the surfaced track as it climbs almost imperceptibly. Kinder Scout, the Derwent Edges, Back Tor and Hollins Cross are all easy to pinpoint if visibility is clear. Within a quarter of a mile ignore the left turn into Rowter Farm and its campsite, choosing instead to continue forwards to a stone step stile by a five-barred gate. The lane, now unsurfaced, embarks on a very gradual descent between the wall on your left and a fence on your right. After a quarter of a mile the fence ends; follow the wall as far as a T-junction.

Turning left into a walled lane, you quickly arrive at a stone step stile by a five-barred gate and a footpath sign with three arms, one pointing to Batham Gate (the Roman road to Buxton), another to Peak Forest and a third to Castleton. Turn left over a second stone step stile adjacent to a five-barred gate, and walk between two walls for a distance of 20 yards; in the absence of a stile, pass to the left of another five-barred gate before veering right as instructed by a small waymarker post. Stay to the left of a white bath and, subsequently, two former railway wagons. Descend to the head of a shallow valley at a point where a wall comes in from the left.

At the Y-junction go right to a small metal gate, its lower half solid, its upper in the form of railings. Maintain direction along the dry, shallow valley, staying to the left of a collapsed stone wall, then negotiate another small metal gate on your way to a Y-junction where the wall swings to the left. Fork right, downhill. From this point the rate of descent quickens, the surface becomes rocky and the valley sides begin to close in with limestone outcrops dotted about the flanks.

Pass between two narrow gateposts to another metal gate. Afterwards the descent steepens even further but offers the first tantalising glimpse of Peveril Castle, perched high above on a limestone outcrop as you continue

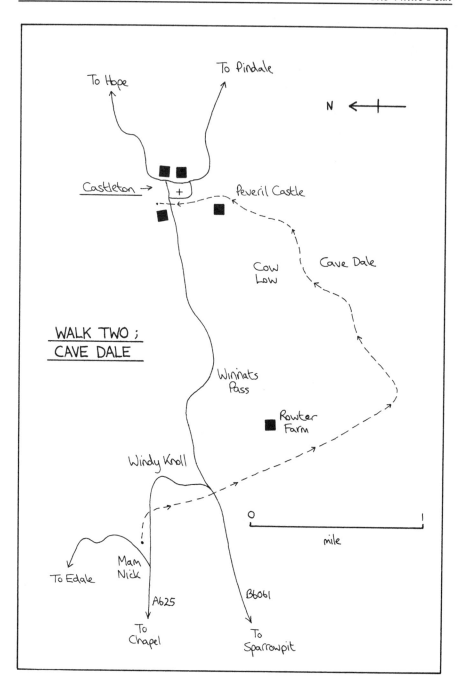

To Hope

To Pindale

N ←——

Castleton →

Peveril Castle

Cave Dale

Cow
Low

WALK TWO ;
CAVE DALE

Winnats
Pass

Rowter
Farm

Windy Knoll

0   1

mile

To Edale

Mam
Nick

A625

B6061

To
Chapel

To
Sparrowpit

through Cave Dale. It is obvious that no attacker would relish the prospect of scaling those heights from this angle with the defenders waiting above.

The path continues through a very narrow rocky defile to a stile alongside a wooden gate. Proceed between cottages for 20 yards and turn left along Pindale Road, which soon becomes Bargate. Walk to the left of the village green with its war memorial before making a right turn into Castle Street to pass the youth hostel and the parish church of St Edmund. At the junction with the A625 turn left down the hill to the car park. If travelling by bus turn right for the bus station.

3. Peakshole

A pleasant riverside amble through grazing meadows with the Great Ridge as your constant companion.

Route: Castleton – Peakshole Water – Hope – Brough – Bamford.

Start: Car park, Castleton village. Map reference 149830. Altitude 197 metres.

Finish: Bus turnaround, Bamford. Map reference 207825. Altitude 150 metres.

Distance: 4¼ miles.

Duration: 2½ hours.

Maps: 1. The Peak District: Dark Peak Area, number 1 in the Ordnance Survey Outdoor Leisure series.
2. Sheffield, Sheet SK 28/38, number 743 in the Ordnance Survey Pathfinder series.

Public Transport: Castleton has a daily bus service from Sheffield and Chesterfield. On summer Sundays and Bank Holidays there are buses from Manchester, Glossop, Rochdale, Ashton, Oldham, Derby, Ashbourne, Mansfield, Bakewell, Barnsley and Buxton. There is a bus from Macclesfield on a limited number of summer Sundays and a bus from Hanley, Leek and Buxton on Saturdays. It is also possible to reach Castleton from Manchester or Sheffield by train, by taking a bus from Hope station. Bamford has frequent daily trains from Manchester, Sheffield and intermediate stations. There are regular daily buses from Sheffield, Castleton and Chesterfield; and buses on summer Sundays and Bank Holidays from Manchester, Glossop, Rochdale, Oldham, Stalybridge, and Ashton.

By Car: Bamford and Castelton are both on the A625 Sheffield–Chapel-en-le-Frith road. Car park in Castleton village. Car park by Bamford station, just off A625.

Refreshments: Cafés and pubs in Castleton and Bamford.

Along the Way

Castleton

See Walk 1.

Hope

Probably the oldest ecclesiastical centre in the entire valley, the village has had a church since Saxon times. Certainly it is the only church mentioned in Domesday Book. The stone cross to be found in the churchyard is believed to date from before the Norman Conquest. The present building dates from the fourteenth century. The small niche above the porch holds a statue of the patron, St Peter.

Brough

There is little visual evidence to show that Brough was once a Roman fort, Navio, built to dominate the local tribes and to protect the lead-mining interests of the Empire. It was a focal point of Roman roads, routes linking it with Templeborough, near Rotherham, Melandra near Glossop and Buxton. Stretches of these ancient highways are still to be found, including Doctor's Gate, the track from Hope to Alport Bridge, and Batham Gate, the road to Buxton.

Bamford

The village was associated with cotton spinning from 1780 until the closure of the last mill in 1965.

The Route

Leaving the car park in Castleton by the main entrance turn left along the A625. Wind your way through the village but, approximately 100 yards beyond the entrance to Weaving Avenue, turn right into a walled lane which soon dispenses with its walls; on the left is Peakshole Water, which started life somewhere inside Peak Cavern.

Over the first stile, stay just to the right of a fence to enjoy a taste of ancient and modern. Peveril Castle, built in 1086, is away to your right while Hope Cement Works, with its tall chimney, is clearly visible directly ahead. The landscape on the left is dominated by the Great Ridge which presents a fantastic skyline – from Mam Tor in the west, through Hollins Cross and Back Tor to Lose Hill in the east.

The path works its way over green pastures dotted with fattening sheep to pass through a broken wall before the tiny river meanders away to your left. By means of stiles cross a narrow field before negotiating a wall gap to a stile which lies 10 yards to the left of a metal gate. Continue forward, staying to

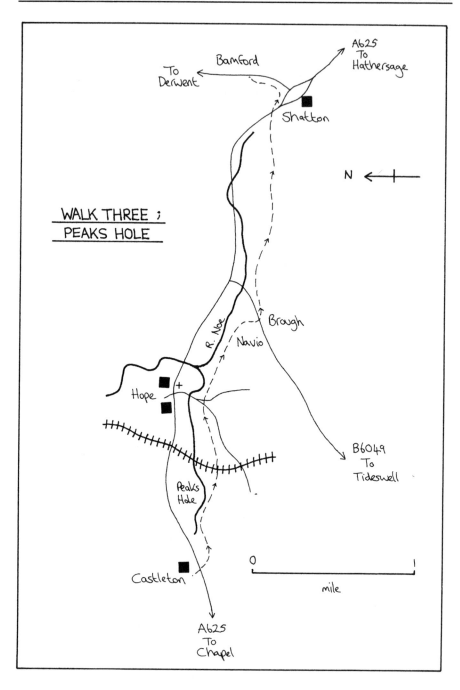

WALK THREE ;
PEAKS HOLE

the left of a small hillock crowned with trees, before veering leftwards along the clear path as it returns to the southern bank of Peakshole Water, passing some gnarled and twisted hawthorns in the process.

Over the next stile use great caution in crossing the railway line to another stile, before continuing forward to the right of several tall trees to a further stile. Traverse the bottom of a meadow which slopes upwards to your right to reach a minor road. There is a handy bench here on which to rest.

Turn left along the road for 20 yards and right into Eccles Lane which is signed to Bradwell. You pass a house on your left and, after 75 yards, make a left turn over a stile to join a footpath signed to Brough. Initially it is a rough track but soon narrows into a traditional path running along a grass terrace studded with molehills; after passing two gateposts on the left you reach a through stile.

Beyond this the path twists its way through a patch of stunted hawthorns before straightening to stay with the boundary fence of a plantation on your right. Below to the left is a prominent campsite. Over the next stile, where the plantation corners away to the right, maintain your line of direction to a footbridge.

At the far end turn left to cross the centre of the field which is the site of the Roman fort of Navio. You will be hard pressed to see any remains. On gaining a stile at the far side veer right down a slope to a Peak and Northern Footpath Society sign by the road from Bradwell to the A625. Turn left for 15 yards and then right into Brough Lane. After a short climb, and where the lane bends acutely to the right, continue forward onto a roughly surfaced track.

Negotiate two stiles in quick succession and pass through a five-barred gate to a Y-junction. Fork right to remain along the broad lane; a wall on the immediate right gives way to a hedge. After a green five-barred gate turn left into a lane; this leads you, after some distance, into the small but attractive hamlet of Shatton.

Using the raised footpath, negotiate the ford to follow the road to the A625. Turn right, passing the High Peak garden centre on your left, and cross the river via the footbridge alongside Mytham Bridge. Just beyond fork left into the road which leads directly to the bus turnaround at Bamford. The station is on the opposite side of the A6013, Station Road.

4. Ford and Bridge

A charming walk, commencing with a steep descent of Abney Clough followed by level walking alongside Highlow Brook to Leadmill Bridge on the outskirts of Hathersage.

Route: Abney – Stoke Ford – Highlow Brook – Leadmill Bridge.

Start: Abney village. Map reference 198799. Altitude 305 metres.

Finish: Leadmill Bridge on the B6001. Map reference 234805. Altitude 137 metres.

Distance: 3 miles.

Duration: 1½ hours.

Maps: 1. The Peak District: White Peak Area, number 24 in the Ordnance Survey Outdoor Leisure series.
2. Sheffield, Sheet SK 28/38, number 743 in the Ordnance Survey Pathfinder series.

Public Transport: Abney has neither buses nor trains.

Hathersage has a frequent daily train service from Manchester and Sheffield. For the railway station continue along the B6001 for almost half a mile from the finish at Leadmill Bridge. Hathersage also has daily buses from Castleton, Sheffield and Chesterfield. Leadmill Bridge has occasional buses from Bakewell, Castleton and Bakewell. There is a bus from Alfreton, Ilkeston and Ripley on summer Sundays and Bank Holidays.

By Car: The village of Abney is reached by a minor road signed from the B6001 just south of Leadmill Bridge. Very restricted roadside parking.

Leadmill Bridge is on the B6001 approximately half a mile to the south of Hathersage. Limited roadside parking. There is a car park in Hathersage.

Refreshments: The Plough Inn by Leadmill Bridge serves bar meals at lunchtime and in the evening. There is a selection of cafés and pubs in Hathersage.

Along the Way

Abney

This is a tiny farming community high on the northern fringe of the White Peak plateau. Nearby, but not on the route, is Highlow Hall, a fine sixteenth-century house (not open to the public) which was once home to the Eyre family.

Stoke Ford

A delightfully serene spot, where the silence is disturbed only by the sound of running water as several streams converge, and the calls of the woodland birds. Ideal for a coffee break or even lunch. It was formerly a rendezvous for packhorse routes.

Stoke Ford

Leadmill Bridge

The Hazelford crossing of the River Derwent has been a vital link in communications for centuries, with a heavy weight in traffic carrying wool to and from Halifax. Originally it was a ford but floods made passage so treacherous that in 1708 an arched bridge was constructed. It was widened in 1928. It takes its name from a mill which once stood nearby.

The Route

From the telephone kiosk in the centre of Abney walk for approximately 100 yards in the direction of Hathersage before turning right by a faded green metal footpath sign indicating a route to Eyam by way of Stoke Ford. Pass through a metal five-barred gate onto a very wide stony track, initially running to the right of a wall.

This soon gives way to trees and, after you have negotiated a rather dilapidated wooden five-barred gate after 200 yards, the track acquires an excellent turf surface so that walking high above Abney Brook is an experience to be savoured. Having made your way through a gateway you continue to descend, with a row of pylons a little way to your right. The flanking slopes are liberally blessed with scattered trees and gorse which, in season, add a sparkling brightness of colour.

Eventually the path levels to run along the contour and between two gateposts to enter woodlands – consisting of hawthorn, wild rose, rowan, hazel and ash – with a good underlayer of bracken and bramble dappled with foxglove. In spring and summer the air is filled with the songs of blue and great tits, chaffinch, willow warbler, chiffchaff, blackbird and other woodland species. In winter you may hear the lone voice of the robin.

By a solitary gatepost the path curves to the right as the pace of descent quickens. You pass under overhead wires and cross several side streams before the next gateway, after which the path transforms itself into a wide track. After yet another gateway, ignore the instructions of a fingered footpath sign and instead swing round to the right along a flagged path for 10 yards, before crossing a small wooden footbridge. Advance a further 10 yards and turn left over a wooden stile to a second and larger footbridge which carries you towards a Peak and Northern Footpath Society sign at Stoke Ford. Litter-conscious walkers will heed the handwritten notices hereabouts and the sharp of eye will spot the confluence of Abney and Bretton Brooks to form Highlow Brook.

Eschew the Peak and Northern sign to Eyam and instead choose a path indicated by a yellow arrow, staying to the left of the sign for a brief climb of some 70 yards with Mill Wood on the far side of the stream. Ahead is a

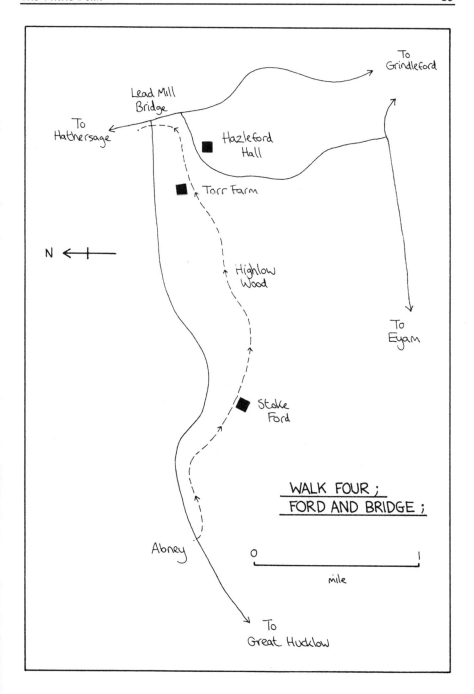

To
Grindleford

Lead Mill
Bridge

To
Hathersage

Hazleford
Hall

Torr Farm

N ←

Highlow
Wood

To
Eyam

Stoke
Ford

WALK FOUR ;
FORD AND BRIDGE ;

Abney

0 ⊢———————————⊣

mile

To
Great Hucklow

breathtaking panorama of bracken-carpeted, rounded slopes which are usually Hovis-brown in autumn. Along this stretch it is also worth noting the evidence of ancient 'pitching', an old technique once again being employed to restore eroded footpaths elsewhere in the Peak District and other National Parks.

Soon the path is out in the open, crossing a stream flowing down from Eyam Moor on your right before veering left a few yards to run between two more gateposts long ago deprived of their intended function. Beyond, climb gradually for 200 yards for a magnificent vista of the rolling hills and side cloughs that make this area so distinctive and so different from other areas of the Peak. Immediately on your right is Bole Hill while to the left is Highlow Bank and High Low.

Soon the springy turf path embarks on a long gentle descent before reaching another Peak and Northern Footpath Society sign, this time indicating the route you have just followed from Stoke Ford and Abney. By using the stepping stones, cross the brook flowing in from your right, to a facing wooden stile. Maintain direction through a new plantation.

Beyond the next five-barred wooden gate Highlow Wood, surrounded by a well-built stone wall, is reached. Proceed to the right of the woods but, by the far corner, swing leftwards through another gateway.

Stay forward just to the right of a wall towards a gate. Look for the gigantic boulder which forms an integral part of the wall just a few yards to the right of it. By the next five-barred gate Torr Farm is on your left. Continue forward along the farm approach track for 200 yards before meeting the road from Eyam to Hathersage. Turn left for the very rapid descent past Hazelford Hall to the B6001. Make a left turn for the remaining 200 yards to Leadmill Bridge, passing, if you have the will power, the Plough Inn on your way. Hathersage station is a further half mile along the B6001 from Leadmill Bridge.

5. Three Villages

Route: Foolow – Eyam – Stoney Middleton.

Start: The village green, Foolow. Map reference 191768. Altitude 295 metres.

Finish: Stoney Middleton. Map reference 231755. Altitude 150 metres.

Distance: 3 miles.

Duration: 1½ hours.

Map: The Peak District: White Peak Area, number 24 in the Ordnance Survey Outdoor Leisure series.

Public Transport: Both Foolow and Stoney Middleton have daily bus services from Manchester, Stockport, Tideswell, Sheffield and Chesterfield.

By Car: Foolow is signed from the A623 east of Wardlow Mires. There is limited parking by the village green. Stoney Middleton is on the A623; parking is difficult except for pub car parks.

Refreshments: The Lazy Landlord in Foolow serves bar meals. There is a choice of pubs and cafés in Eyam (midway) and in Stoney Middleton.

Along the Way

Foolow

A tiny village of mellow stone houses and cottages, Foolow is clustered round its picturesque green and pond or mere. The Hall, now converted into two houses, is remarkable for its mullioned windows and dates from the seventeenth century. The Manor House, with its facade of three bay windows, was built a century later. Other old houses are the Spread Eagle, formerly, as its name implies, an eighteenth-century pub, and The Nook, from the sixteenth century. The tiny church and chapel are of more recent origin, having been built in Victorian times.

There is a medieval cross by the green and a very unusual Bull Ring. Now noted for its pastoral farming, Foolow was once involved in lead-mining, the Watergrove Mine ceasing operations in 1853. Its chimney stood as a landmark until it was demolished in 1960.

Foolow: Pinfold, Mere and Cross

Eyam

Known internationally as 'The Plague Village', Eyam was one of the few places outside London to experience the Great Plague of 1665–66, although sporadic outbreaks of the disease were not unknown in most areas during that period. The disaster started when a widow, Mary Cooper, took in a lodger, George Viccars. A tailor by profession, he received a consignment of clothes from London, which proved to be contaminated.

Soon Viccars was dead and the mortality rate escalated as the fatal disease obtained a firm hold. Led by the vicar, William Mompesson, the villagers agreed to a self-imposed quarantine whereby nobody was to leave. Arrangements were made for supplies of food to be deposited at certain fixed points on the outskirts of Eyam, much of the cost being borne by the Duke of Devonshire. The church was closed, and services were held instead in Cucklet Delph to the south of the village.

There was a temporary respite during the winter but the number of deaths increased in 1666. The final victim died in November, bringing the total death toll to 260 out of a population variously estimated at between 300 and 700. Eyam holds a commemorative service in Cucklet Delph on the final Sunday of August every year.

There are several other reminders of the disaster including Plague Cottages and the graves of various victims, who were usually interred well away from habitation.

Sundial, Eyam Church

The plague apart, Eyam has several attractions to commend it. The Hall, constructed in 1671, has been in the possession of the Wright family ever since. It is open to the public during the summer. The exact age of the parish church is impossible to determine, although parts are thought to have existed since Saxon times. The present structure is twelfth-century. The pulpit is Jacobean as is the chair to the right of the altar. Both were used by Mompesson before and after the plague.

On the exterior south wall of the church is a most unusual sundial. It was made by a local mason, William Shaw, in 1775. Not only does it show the time in half hours but it also gives local times for Rome, Bermuda, Mecca, Jerusalem and other places around the globe. It is decorated with the signs of the zodiac.

Like many White Peak villages, Eyam was associated with lead-mining for centuries. Fluorspar extraction is still carried on. With the advent of the Industrial Revolution cotton mills made their appearance, to be replaced later by silk. When these declined the manufacture of shoes took over but, sadly, the last pair was produced in 1979.

Stoney Middleton

The car driver passing through Stoney Middleton on the busy A623 may be forgiven for thinking of it as an unprepossessing place but, away from the main road, it has many attractive stone cottages and quaint corners.

Its small church is one of the most unusual not only in Derbyshire but in the country. At the time when the Romans were flocking to Buxton to partake of the waters, Stoney Middleton also boasted its own bath. During the Dark Ages and the medieval period the spring that fed this bath became a shrine for those in search of a miraculous cure. A tiny chapel dedicated to St Martin was built and stood until the village became a parish in its own right in 1743. Apart from the tower, built by Joan Eyre to mark her husband's return from the crusades, the building was demolished and replaced by a strange octagonal church with columns carrying the lantern, with the result that there is an internal ambulatory.

The Hall, built in or about 1600, has a twin-gabled facade while on the A623 there is an octagonal toll house surviving from the turnpike era.

Not far from the village centre along Middleton Dale is 'Lover's Leap' from where, in 1762, Hannah Baddaley threw herself off the top of the rocks because her boyfriend had deserted her. Fortunately, her voluminous skirt acted as a parachute and she landed safely.

Middleton appears to have always been closely associated with industry. Lead-mining, quarrying, shoe manufacture and smelting have all taken place there. It is also noted as a rock climbing centre.

The Route

Leave Foolow village green by walking eastwards towards the road junction. The Lazy Landlord pub is on your left. Strike out along the road to

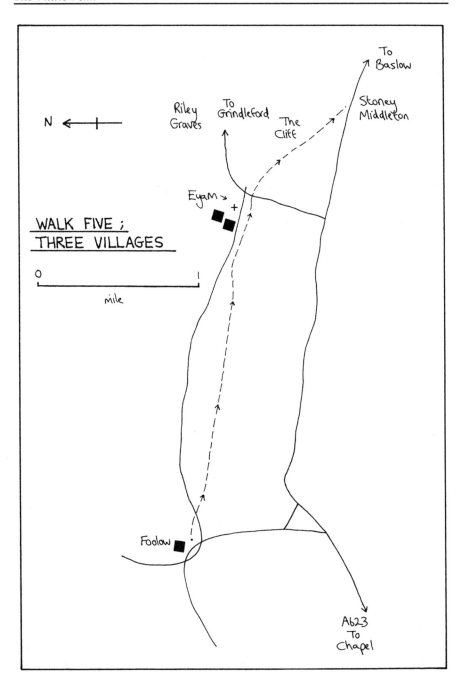

N ← |

Riley
Graves

To
Grindleford

The
Cliff

To
Baslow

Stoney
Middleton

Eyam →
+

WALK FIVE ;
THREE VILLAGES

0   1

mile

Foolow

A623
To
Chapel

Eyam but, having passed a pinfold on your right, and by the Foolow village sign, turn right over a stile with a footpath finger post alongside. Cross the field diagonally left, aiming for a small stone barn and a squeezer stile in the wall on your left.

Turn through this to advance – with the barn on your immediate right – to a second squeezer stile within 15 yards. Keep to the left of a wall and, after a stone step stile, cross the next field to a broken stone step stile (where I came across a lady who had slipped on the stile and broken her leg).

In summer the meadow cranesbill are profuse here while the skylark serenades perpetually overhead. Away to your left is Eyam Edge with the Barrel Inn at Bretton conspicuous on the skyline.

Remaining to the left of a wall, proceed to the next stone step stile before dipping slightly to a squeezer stile in Linen Dale. Go forward 20 yards to a footpath post and another stone step stile before climbing gently and veering slightly left, passing beneath some overhead wires.

Go through a wall gap and maintain direction to a stile by a footpath finger post pointing the way to Eyam. Work your way between several grassed-over spoil heaps – evidence of past industry – before the next wall gap provides passage to another sign. Maintaining the same line of direction traverse open pasture to find, after yet another wall gap, a wall on your right. Negotiate a stone step stile to the right of two small blue metal five-barred gates, cross a narrow lane and, guided by a series of stiles, stay forward until the descent towards the village of Eyam, which is now in view ahead.

After crossing more fields in a virtually straight line, walk between two garden hedges with a bungalow on your right. Go down a short flight of stone steps on to a surfaced lane, cross to a stile and walk over the next field to a narrow road. Again cross directly to a squeezer stile before advancing between a hedge on your left and a fence and the White House on your right.

Continue through a new housing estate and New Close until meeting Church Street in the centre of Eyam. Turn right, passing the green with its stocks opposite the Hall and, subsequently, Plague Cottages and the church, to arrive at the junction of Church Street with the B6521.

Proceed cautiously across the centre of the junction to enter Lydgate, climbing steadily between stone cottages and by a small walled enclosure containing the graves of some plague victims. Lydgate was formerly the main road into the village, where a nightly watch was mounted to interrogate approaching visitors.

Where the road bends round to the left, and by the end of the houses, pass through a facing squeezer stile to the immediate right of a wooden five-barred gate, where a footpath finger post points the way to Stoney Middleton.

The appropriately stony track has a second five-barred gate within 100 yards but the path goes round the right-hand side rather than through it, and then picks up a wall on the right. By the next footpath post go left through a squeezer stile to walk between two walls about 3 yards apart. Your route is flanked by nettles, wild roses, red campion and meadow cranesbill. Pass between two derelict barns 100 yards apart to enjoy a good though distant view of the Riley Graves on the slopes far to your left; this is the burial place of several members of the Hancock family, all plague victims.

After the next squeezer stile aim a little to the right of a prominent clump of trees with a view of a large quarry face some 100 yards to the right. By the centre of this large expanse of grassland veer right into a shallow depression before commencing the ever-steepening descent of 'The Cliff', to reach a footpath sign at the bottom of the hill pointing towards Eyam. Climb the nearby stile, turn right down the road to a junction and go left to pass the church of St Martin and the river before making an exit onto the A623. The bus stop is to the right.

6. The Gibbet

A charming short walk offering an amazing array of skylines and passing one of the most unusual rock formations in the National Park. *This walk should not be attempted alone by people of a nervous disposition.*

Route: Litton – Tansley Dale – Cressbrook Dale – St Peter's Stone – Wardlow Mires.

Start: The village green, Litton. Map reference 164752. Altitude 300 metres.

Finish: Wardlow Mires. Map reference 181756. Altitude 235 metres.

Distance: 1¾ miles.

Duration: 1–1½ hours.

Map: The Peak District: White Peak Area, number 24 in the Ordnance Survey Outdoor Leisure series.

Public Transport: Litton has buses from Manchester, Stockport, Chesterfield, Sheffield and Buxton daily. There are buses from Bakewell daily except Sunday, from Castleton on Tuesdays, Thursdays and Fridays and from Rochdale, Ashton and Glossop on summer Sundays and Bank Holidays.

Wardlow Mires has buses from Manchester, Stockport and Chesterfield daily. Buses from Bakewell daily except Sunday.

By Car: Litton is reached by a minor road signed from the A623 west of Wardlow Mires and from the B6049 south of Tideswell. There is limited parking around the village green. Wardlow Mires is on the A623 but there is very little roadside parking.

Refreshments: The Red Lion at Litton serves bar meals. The Mires café at Wardlow Mires is open 7am–7pm.

Along the Way

Litton

The main street of Litton is wide, lined with grass verges, and terminates in the triangular village green at the western end. Many of the houses bear date stones, the earliest being 1639, although most are of the eighteenth century when lead-mining was a flourishing industry. Clergy House and Hammerton House are the two most outstanding but most are typical of the vernacular architecture of the area. The church dates from 1929.

Litton: 18th-century house

Cressbrook Dale

The upper section of Cressbrook Dale is a National Nature Reserve owned by English Nature. Its rich and varied limestone flora is subject to a strict grazing regime.

St Peter's Stone

This unusually shaped limestone rock, visible from the A623, obtained its name because of its similarity to the dome of St Peter's Church in Rome. It may require this spiritual protection because strange, unworldly happenings have been reported in its vicinity. Shortly before this book was written a friend of mine, a sober, down-to-earth chap, experienced weird feelings when he climbed to the top with his son. Although only separated by a few yards, neither could hear the other shouting. Other visitors claim to have felt unseen hands encircling their necks, even in broad daylight.

Even without these strange experiences St Peter's Stone was the setting for a macabre event in the last century. On New Year's Day 1815, Hannah Oliver, a toll-gate keeper at Wardlow Mires, was brutally murdered. Subsequently 21-year-old Anthony Lingard of Tideswell was tried for the crime, convicted and hanged. As was the practice in those days, his corpse was suspended from a gibbet on the top of St Peter's Stone as a warning to others of the retribution that comes the way of murderers.

I will leave you to make your own decisions as to whether there are any connections between the known facts and the eerie experiences of later visitors.

Wardlow Mires

Wardlow Mires, now on the A623 Chapel-en-le-Frith to Chesterfield road, has been on a major transport route from prehistoric times. Long before the Romans conquered these islands it was served by the Old Portway, a track linking various hill forts throughout the Peak District. In medieval times saltways from Cheshire to the east passed by and it was well-known to jaggers and drovers. Not surprisingly the road was later turnpiked and it is still one of the vital trans-Pennine arteries.

The Route

From the village green walk along the broad main street in the direction signed to Wardlow and Cressbrook, passing the Clergy House with its plaque 'W. M. 1723' on your left and 'The Old Co-op' on your right. Part way along the street make a right turn into the very narrow road signposted to Cressbrook and Monsal Dale. Take a close look at Hall Cottages on your left and pause awhile to take a backward glance at Litton Edge which protects the village from the north.

After approximately 250 yards, and where the road bends round through 90 degrees to the right, turn left into a walled lane. Again, after a further 250 yards, and by a finger post, turn over a stone step stile on your right.

Veer diagonally left towards another very obvious footpath sign by a wall corner. This section of our route affords an excellent opportunity for studying the field system surrounding Litton and for viewing Eyam Edge and Wardlow Hay Cop, with its Triangulation Pillar at 370 metres. Round the wall corner leftwards, and still veering left on the remarkably distinct path,

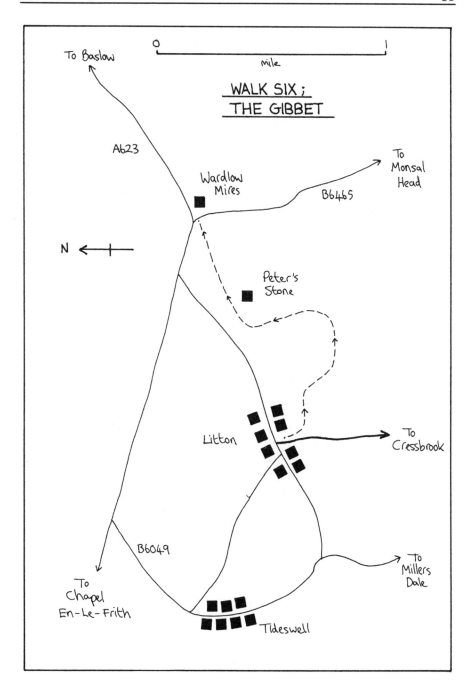

WALK SIX;
THE GIBBET

aim for a second wall corner part way down the slope. By this corner make a sharp left turn to a wooden stile after only four yards.

An English Nature notice, a few yards beyond the stile, announces entry to Cressbrook Dale National Nature Reserve combined with a request to respect the flora. You are also advised not to stray too far from the path because of the risk of disappearing down dangerous mine shafts.

From these signs veer right down the slope towards a short section of wall and hawthorn. Stay to the left of the wall as the serious descent begins with a dramatic view into the length of Tansley Dale. On reaching the valley floor, the bare flanks rearing on either side show only a scattering of hawthorns but in high summer they put on a fine display of harebells, meadow cranesbill, red campion and other flowers.

At the junction of Tansley Dale with Cressbrook Dale climb a facing wooden stile, cross the stream by the carefully arranged stepping stones, turn left and walk to the right of the clear stream and the wall beyond. This is an idyllic spot, a place to rest and contemplate, while gazing towards the dramatic limestone escarpments.

Although you are now walking upstream the rate of ascent is almost imperceptible. The enclosing flanks are extremely steep and the valley narrow. Through a wall gap the path becomes wider while acquiring a turf surface which is gentle on the feet. Eventually the path rounds the western base of St Peter's Stone, after which the valley becomes noticeably shallower. Just after another English Nature notice a walled lane develops, which passes through a five-barred wooden gate. Stay to the left of Brook Side Farm to exit by the junction of the A623 with the B6465 at Wardlow Mires.

7. Dales Way

This walk descends gradually through a succession of four limestone dales. For the most part the walking is easy and gentle but the final stretch through Monk's Dale is very stony and can be muddy after wet weather.

Route: Peak Forest – Dam Dale – Hay Dale – Peter Dale – Monk's Dale.

Start: By the church, Peak Forest. Map reference 114792. Altitude 316 metres.

Finish: By the church, Miller's Dale. Map reference 141733. Altitude 220 metres.

Distance: 5 miles.

Duration: 3 hours.

Map: The Peak District: White Peak Area, number 24 in the Ordnance Survey Outdoor Leisure series.

Public Transport: Peak Forest is served by daily buses from Chesterfield, Stockport and Manchester. One bus only from Castleton on Tuesdays, Thursdays and Fridays.

Miller's Dale has daily buses from Buxton, Tideswell, Chesterfield and Sheffield. On summer Sundays and Bank Holidays there are buses from Barnsley, Buxton, Bakewell, Castleton, Mansfield, Derby and Ashbourne.

By Car: Peak Forest is on the A623. Limited parking away from the main road.

Miller's Dale is approached by the B6049 which runs from the A623 at Tideswell Moor to the A6 near Taddington. There is a National Park car park on the site of the former railway station.

Refreshments: The Devonshire Arms opposite the start of the walk at Peak Forest serves bar meals. Bar food is available at the Angler's Rest about 100 yards down the minor road signed to Litton Mill at the end of the walk. There is a café opposite the car park in Miller's Dale.

Along the Way

Peak Forest

Technically inside the Forest of the High Peak, this village has fewer trees than most. Yet, in the olden days, courts to enforce the forest laws were held here in what is now Chamber Farm, close by Chamber Knoll.

Its greatest claim to fame, however, is its reputation as a Gretna Green of the Peak District. In 1657 when Oliver Cromwell and the Puritans ruled the land, Christian, Countess of Devonshire defied them all by building a private chapel here dedicated to King Charles the Martyr. She and her chapel survived but the vicar claimed that he was outside the jurisdiction of the bishop, and as a result was entitled to perform marriage ceremonies at any hour of night or day.

This practice continued until 1753 when an Act of Parliament made it illegal to perform marriages outside the hours of daylight. Nevertheless, clandestine marriages took place at Peak Forest until as late as 1804. The present church dates from 1877.

Mill Wheel, Miller's Dale

Miller's Dale

Miller's Dale takes its name from the corn mill erected here during the reign of King John. Over the centuries it appears to have been rebuilt several times. The final building has served a variety of purposes in recent years.

When the railway was built through Monsal Dale to Manchester, Miller's Dale became an important junction for passengers changing for Buxton which, as a result, enjoyed a boom as a spa town. It was the only station in the country with a post office on the platform. Today it is a car park.

The Route

From the church head along the A625 in an easterly direction. Opposite the Devonshire Arms turn right into Damside Lane; you soon pass a recreation ground on your left and the unusually named Candlemas Cottage facing it. Beyond Damside Farm the lane degenerates into a rough track.

A little way past the farm and before a cottage turn left to a Peak and Northern Footpath Society sign. Ten yards further make a right turn to a stone step stile and pass the side of a cottage to re-join the original track. Turn left with a double five-barred gate to your right. Where the track terminates veer right over a field to a ladder stile and Dam Dale Farm. Keep to the left of the farm boundary wall to reach a small wooden gate after approximately 40 yards. Continue forwards between a wall on your right and a rock outcrop on your left to enter Dam Dale proper which, at this point, is a wide, shallow valley with sporadic patches of red campion, and cattle grazing the adjacent fields.

The clear, well-used path runs through a wall gap to a stile followed by two more wall gaps in quick succession and a wooden stile. Before the next stile is reached there is a stone barn to your right, reminiscent of those in the Yorkshire Dales, which in turn, is overlooked by Losehill Farm from the top of the flanking slope.

Maintain direction along the valley floor, still with a wall on your right, and resisting all temptation to veer left up an apparent track to your left. Your path pursues its relentless course through yet another wall gap and over another stile until coming face-to-face with a long and formidable-looking limestone outcrop. Do not lose heart. You do not have to climb it!

Instead, negotiate the stone step stile at its base into a walled lane. Turn right so that the outcrop is now on your left. Within a short distance, and by a stand of trees, a T-junction is reached as another walled lane comes in from the right. Keep forward over a facing wooden stile to wander through an avenue of deciduous trees rich in fungi. The wide, grassy path loses height gradually, leading you past a small defunct quarry with its abandoned equipment.

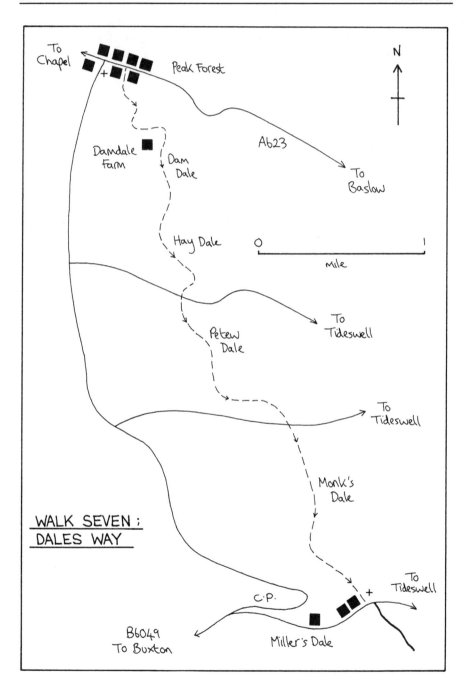

To
Chapel

Peak Forest

N

Damdale
Farm

Dam
Dale

Ab23

To
Baslow

Hay Dale

0   mile   1

To
Tideswell

Peter
Dale

To
Tideswell

Monk's
Dale

WALK SEVEN :
DALES WAY

To
Tideswell

C.P.

B6049
To Buxton

Miller's Dale

Further down Hay Dale the trees are replaced by scattered, scrubby haw-thorn as the flanking slopes steepen and, beyond a stone step stile where the valley curves to the right, there are walls on either side. A further stretch of trees resounds to the calls of robin, blackbird, thrush, and green woodpecker while in front an impressive miniature range of limestone tors comes into view.

Over the next wooden stile the minor road from Wheston is reached at Dale Head. Turn right along the road for 30 yards and then go left over a stone step stile to enter Peter Dale. Once again the path is broad with a springy turf surface, making walking a real pleasure as we wind our way through a veritable sea of nettles and ragwort before passing between two wooden gateposts marked with the logo of the Limestone Way – a ram's head.

Once again the route is flanked by stone walls and the next solitary gatepost is waymarked with a white arrow. Beyond, the dale widens briefly, before the path goes between another pair of gateposts to enter a narrow, rocky defile for a distance of 100 yards. Having crossed a large pasture where cows normally graze, a combination of a wooden and stone step stile allows passage onto the Tideswell–Hargatewall road.

Cross directly to a squeezer stile for the entry into Monk's Dale, a name which is a reminder that many of the great monastic houses on the fringe of the Peak District owned extensive sheep ranches or granges within its boundaries. Initially Monk's Dale is wide and open but, after the first 100 yards, it narrows into a steep sided and well-wooded valley. A squeezer stile allows entry into Monk's Dale National Nature Reserve, which is managed by English Nature for its trees and flora including red campion, ragged robin, ground ivy and many other species, some of which are very rare.

The path, still clear and gradually descending, is rocky so that care is needed in placing the feet. After wet weather it is usually very muddy. There are occasional openings, but the moss-covered rocks are testimony to the gen-eral dampness of the valley. Following a brief stretch where height is lost more rapidly, pass through another squeezer stile and twist left for a short climb of 50 yards before turning right to walk just above the tree line alongside a derelict wall. At the end of 100 yards descend back into the woods before finally emerging into an impressive steep-sided valley. At this stage the going is easier as the path traverses pasture with a stream to your right.

On meeting another path by a boulder, turn right to climb slightly by a yellow waymarker as the valley curves gracefully to the right. In no time at all the path drops back into the open valley with a view of the southern flank of Miller's Dale directly in front, signalling that journey's end is close at hand.

Turn right over the wooden footbridge and, at the far end, turn left to walk through more scrub until meeting another English Nature notice. Proceed forward 10 yards to a small gate and a surfaced path, which passes between walls and behind a low-roofed cottage to emerge onto the B6049 in Miller's Dale by the church of St Anne; there is a large waterwheel on the opposite side of the road.

The bus stop is close at hand but for the car park turn right and follow the signs.

8. Palatial Splendour

Little more than a gentle stroll through rolling parkland by the banks of the River Derwent.

Route: Baslow – Chatsworth House – Chatsworth Mill – Beeley Bridge.

Start: The car park, Nether Baslow. Map reference 258721. Altitude 110 metres.

Finish: Beeley Bridge on the B6012. Map reference 261684. Altitude 100 metres.

Distance: 2½ miles.

Duration: 1½ hours.

Map: The Peak District: White Peak Area, number 24 in the Ordnance Survey Outdoor Leisure series.

Public Transport: Baslow has daily buses from Manchester, Stockport, Sheffield, Chesterfield, Bakewell, Buxton, Leek and Hanley.

Beeley Bridge has buses from Bakewell on Mondays and Fridays and from Ilkeston, Matlock, Rochdale, Oldham, Ashton and Glossop on summer Sundays and Bank Holidays.

By Car: Baslow is at the junction of the A623, A621 and A619 roads to Chapel-en-le-Frith, Chesterfield, Sheffield and Bakewell. There is a large car park by the bus station at Nether End.

Beeley Bridge is at the southern end of Chatsworth Park on the B6012. There is no immediate parking but just to the north, and signed from the B6012, is the car park at Calton Lees.

Refreshments: There is a selection of cafés and pubs serving meals in Baslow. Part way through the walk is the Carriage House Restaurant at Chatsworth House serving meals and light refreshments. (Open late March–end October 11am–4.30pm.) There is also a refreshment kiosk at Calton Lees car park.

Along the Way

Baslow

Baslow is a busy, bustling village of attractive stone houses situated at one of the key road junctions in the eastern Peak District. Because of its crossings of the River Derwent it has been a centre of communications for centuries. By its three-arched seventeenth-century bridge is a small toll house with a doorway only $3\frac{1}{2}$ feet in height.

The clock on the church tower is most unusual if not unique because it has dispensed with the customary numerals. They have been replaced by 'VICTORIA 1897', in commemoration of the monarch's Diamond Jubilee. Inside the church is a whip, formerly used to drive out stray dogs during Divine Service.

Beeley Bridge

Chatsworth House

The present Chatsworth House is not the first to occupy the site. This was a Tudor building, completed in 1555 for that formidable lady, Bess of Hardwick. Widowed at the advanced age of 15, she had chosen William Cavendish as her second spouse. She chose wisely because he had grown rich by helping Henry VIII to dissolve the monasteries and had shared in the loot.

Splendid by the standards of its time, the Tudor house faced in the opposite direction to the present house which replaced it in 1708. The builder was another William Cavendish, created Duke of Devonshire by William III for his support in driving James II from the English throne. The only part of Bess of Hardwick's house still to be seen is the Hunting Tower, standing on the wooded hillside overlooking the present Chatsworth. The landscaped park was laid out to the designs of Capability Brown.

The interior is so full of artistic treasures that this is not the place to single out any individual item but to suggest a visit in the course of this walk. Chatsworth House is open daily to the public 11am–4.30pm from late March to the end of October.

Chatsworth Mill

Designed in the classical style as an integral part of the estate's architecture, the corn mill was in operation until 1950. It was badly damaged during a gale some 12 years afterwards but is now preserved as a romantic ruin.

The Route

On exiting the car park at Baslow Nether End turn right to a road junction within a few yards. Continue forwards, staying to the right of the Baslow Tea Rooms before crossing an old stone bridge spanning Bar Brook. At the far end and by the footpath finger post, make a right turn, walking with the brook on your right and passing a thatched cottage on your left. This is a most unusual sight in the Peak District.

The track starts life as a walled lane but very soon has a hedge on the left while retaining the wall on the right. Staying with the track, corner a substantial stone house to the left before passing through a high metal kissing gate to enter Chatsworth Park.

Maintain the same line of direction along the chatter track through open parkland dotted with majestic trees. Apart from foxglove by the river along with thistle, clover and buttercup, there is not a single wild flower to be seen. It is a landscape which contrasts sharply with all others in the National Park.

At the next T-junction turn left along a narrow, metalled road to another junction by a strange-looking and oddly shaped white and blue building. Stay forward, now on an unsurfaced track, with the estate nursery on the right and, just beyond that, the confluence of Bar Brook with the River Derwent.

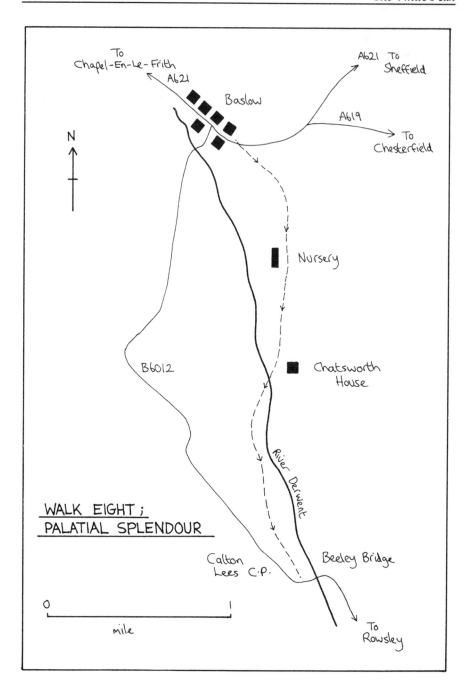

To
Chapel-En-Le-Frith
A621

A621 To
Sheffield

Baslow

A619

To
Chesterfield

N

Nursery

B6012

Chatsworth
House

River Derwent

WALK EIGHT ;
PALATIAL SPLENDOUR

Calton
Lees C.P.

Beeley Bridge

0   1

mile

To
Rowsley

For approximately a quarter mile there is a well-built and high stone wall to your right and, where this ends, it is replaced by a metal fence. By the next intersection of estate tracks still continue forwards with the River Derwent, complete with mallards, moorhen and coot, a little to your right. To your left is a square stone building with ornamental balustrades which was obviously once surrounded by water in the form of a moat.

Fifty yards after this negotiate a small wooden gate before continuing a further 80 yards to meet the main approach road to Chatsworth House which is a little distance to your left. Turn right over the elegant arched bridge and then immediately make a left turn onto the path which traverses the grassland while taking aim for an obvious bend in the River Derwent.

By this bend swing right towards some trees before returning to the western bank of the river by a weir. After a second weir the derelict Chatsworth Mill is on your right. Proceed for the short distance remaining to leave Chatsworth Park onto the B6012 by a metal kissing gate. The return to Calton Lees car park may be made either by turning right along the road or by retracing your steps but forking to the left of the mill to reach the B6012 by the car park entrance.

9. Alpine Style

A short walk across verdant, Alpine type meadows to enjoy a feeling of being 'on top of the world'.

Route: Ballcross Farm – Moatless Plantation – Calton Pastures – New Piece Wood – Edensor.

Start: Ballcross Farm, on the minor road linking Bakewell with Pilsley. Map reference 228694. Altitude 270 metres.

Finish: Edensor village. Map reference 252700. Altitude 120 metres.

Distance: 3 miles.

Duration: 1½ hours.

Map: The Peak District: White Peak Area, number 24 in the Ordnance Survey Outdoor Leisure series.

Public Transport: None to the start.

Edensor has buses from Bakewell on Mondays and Fridays only. On summer Sundays and Bank Holidays there are buses from Ilkeston, Matlock, Rochdale, Oldham, Ashton and Glossop.

By Car: Ballcross Farm is best approached from Bakewell by crossing the bridge on the A619 and turning right at the first road junction to continue climbing beyond the former railway station for approximately one mile. Little roadside parking.

Edensor is on the B6012 Baslow–Rowsley road within Chatsworth Park.

Refreshments: The Post Office and Stables Tea Room, Edensor.

Along the Way

Edensor

Despite appearances, Edensor (pronounced 'Ensor') is a very ancient village, earning a mention in Domesday as 'Edensoure'. During the eighteenth century the Duke of Devonshire, anxious to improve the view from the windows of Chatsworth, had parts of the village wiped out, moving the inhabitants to a new village at Pilsley. During the following century the remaining houses were demolished to be replaced by a carefully planned estate village in a mixture of styles including Gothic, Tudor, Renaissance and Swiss. Paxton, designer of Crystal Palace, was the architect. One of the few buildings to survive was the Chatsworth Institute, formerly the local pub.

Edensor church owes its design to Sir George Gilbert Scott (1811–78), and is in the Early English style. Several members of the Devonshire family are buried there including Lord Frederick Cavendish, Irish Secretary, who was murdered in Phoenix Park, Dublin, in 1882, during a previous round of Irish troubles. In the churchyard is a memorial to the sister of President Kennedy who was married to the Duke's son, Lord Hartington, and died in a plane crash.

Stone-built house, Edensor

The Route

A few yards east (uphill) of Ballcross Farm, leave the road by turning right through a five-barred gate which appears to be permanently open with a footpath finger post propped up against a tree (at least it was when I passed).

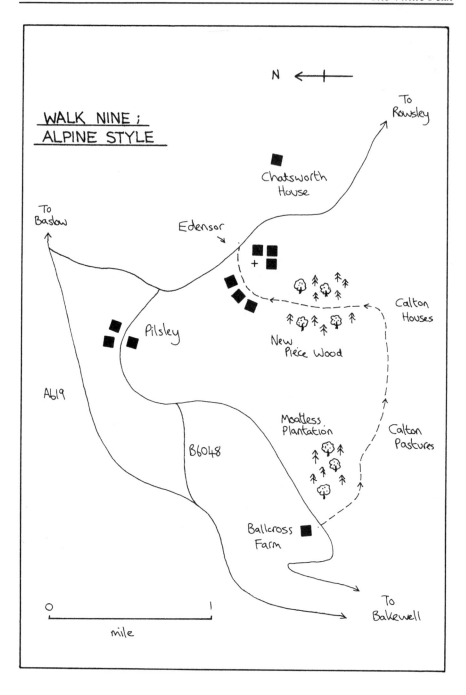

N ←

To
Rowsley

WALK NINE;
ALPINE STYLE

To
Baslow

Chatsworth
House

Edensor

Calton
Houses

New
Piece Wood

Pilsley

A619

Moatless
Plantation

Calton
Pastures

B6048

Ballcross
Farm

To
Bakewell

0   1

mile

Advance to a stile adjacent to another five-barred gate before reaching a junction.

Turn right to a second junction within 100 yards. Make another right turn along a much wider path as it runs along the 280-metre contour and passes to the right of Moatless Plantation. Beyond, it swings right while losing altitude gradually towards a solitary tree. From there maintain the same line of direction by a second lonely tree to a footpath finger post.

There, negotiate the stile in the wire fence and continue to a Y-junction. Fork left, keeping just to the right of a small, nameless mere in following a path signed to Chatsworth. After 100 yards a second stile is reached. Over that let a waymarker post guide you across a very large expanse of Alpine-style upland meadow. Known as Calton Pastures, it is enclosed by New Piece Wood to your left and Manners Wood away to your right. This is a vast green upland amphitheatre, where walking is a joy in summer as swallows dart hither and thither overhead, giving a feeling of being high in the mountains. Having passed through a gateway and to the left of Calton Plantations the path forms a T-junction with a track by a footpath finger post. Turn left in the direction signed Edensor and Chatsworth.

Initially the track climbs slightly with an open-sided hay barn on your right and the roofs of Calton Houses peeping above a fold in the land. Within 100 yards negotiate a stone step stile alongside a five-barred gate to enter New Piece Wood, a blend of coniferous and broad-leaved trees with a mix of rhododendron. The very broad track is flanked by stone walls. The walk through the woods is brief because you exit over another stone step stile after a mere 200 yards.

Pause awhile to admire the view directly in front of you. It is breathtaking, encompassing as it does the village of Edensor, Chatsworth House and Park and, as a backcloth to both, the Eastern Edges.

Perhaps with some reluctance, push forward along the easily recognised path as it descends the grassy slope, taking your line of direction from the steeple of Edensor church. After 100 yards pass a small wooden post and, after a further 100, stay immediately to the left of a wire-enclosed plantation from which emanates the call of the pheasant.

By the far corner of this plantation veer left towards the left-hand corner of a second plantation, crossing a narrow path running along the contour on your way. Maintain your general line of direction with the second plantation on your right, and where this ends continue downwards to pass a solitary oak tree on your left and, further on, a row of six oaks to your right. With these behind you head towards the corner of a fence and wall which is now clearly visible. By this turn left so that there is a house garden on your right.

Where this wall ends veer left away from the continuing fence for 60 yards to a wooden post. Turn right here for 50 yards to a short flight of steps surmounted by a small metal gate set against a most unusual squeezer stile. Descend four steps, advance 12 yards with a fence on your right and a wall on your left before going down a longer flight of steps.

At the bottom turn right down more steps to emerge onto a road by a footpath finger post. Turn right to pass Edensor church on your right and several cottages with colourful gardens before reaching the B6012.

10. To the West End

A gentle stroll through pastures.

Route: Pilsley – Rymas Brook – West End – Baslow.

Start: The road junction by Chatsworth Farm Shop, Pilsley. Map reference 242709. Altitude 191 metres.

Finish: Car park, Nether End, Baslow. Map reference 258721. Altitude 110 metres.

Distance: 2¼ miles.

Duration: 1½ hours.

Map: The Peak District: White Peak Area, number 24 in the Ordnance Survey Outdoor Leisure series.

Public Transport: Pilsley has buses from Chesterfield and Bakewell daily except Sundays. On summer Sundays and Bank Holidays there are buses from Rochdale, Ashton, Glossop, Chesterfield, Sheffield, Dronfield, Buxton and Bakewell. Occasional Sunday buses from Macclesfield.

Baslow has daily buses from Manchester, Stockport, Sheffield, Chesterfield, Buxton, Bakewell, Hanley and Leek.

By Car: Pilsley is on the B6048 between Baslow and Bakewell. There is no official car park but some space around the village green.

Baslow is at the junction of the A619, A621 and A623 roads to Chapel-en-le-Frith, Sheffield, Chesterfield and Bakewell. There is a large car park adjacent to the bus station at Nether End.

Refreshments: The Devonshire Arms in Pilsley village serves bar meals. There is a coffee shop at the Chatsworth Farm Shop in Pilsley near the start. There is a wide selection of hotels, pubs and cafés in Baslow.

Along the Way

Pilsley

At the start of this walk is the Chatsworth Farm Shop where a wide variety of produce from the estate may be purchased. It is housed in the former horse stud farm and one of the buildings contains a craft workshop. Those in need of sustenance for this walk may like to patronise the coffee shop before striding out.

Contrary to what is often said and written about Pilsley, it is not entirely the creation of Joseph Paxton when, during the nineteenth century, the Duke of Devonshire decided to obliterate the existing village of Edensor because it marred the landscaped view from his palatial Chatsworth House. Opposite the Devonshire Arms is a collection of older cottages built between 1709 and 1753 – a reminder that the village has a long history as an agricultural settlement.

When Edensor was demolished, those inhabitants who could not be accommodated in the rebuilt village were transferred to a kind of overspill, again specially designed by Paxton, at Pilsley. It is an attractive village with its own green, and in summer the cottage gardens are a blaze of colour.

Well dressing, Baslow

Baslow

See Walk 8.

The Route

This walk is very unusual, especially for the White Peak, in that it is possible to see the final destination at the outset although it does disappear from view as we make our way towards it. The views from Pilsley encourage one to linger because they embrace not only Baslow but Curbar and Froggat Edges plus the area around Stoney Middleton, including those enormous quarries, and the far more attractive middle reaches of the Derwent Valley.

From the bus stop by the Farm Shop take the road signed to Pilsley. It passes, firstly, the school and then the village green on your left, in addition to several mellow stone houses with attractive flower-filled gardens.

By the Devonshire Arms turn right to pass a furniture showroom. 200 yards beyond the last house, and opposite a stone barn, turn left over an unsigned and obscure stone step stile beneath a large tree. Stay to the left of the wall to be guided by a row of pylons part way along the field. By the wall corner turn right over another stone step stile followed, within 30 yards, by a wooden stile.

Over that veer left, still with the line of pylons, to drop down a steep slope which is dotted with purple orchids in summer. At the bottom pass through a squeezer stile before a tiny footbridge carries you over Rymas Brook to the A619.

Taking great care because visibility is very restricted on this busy road, cross directly to a footpath finger post, footbridge and wooden stile. Veer diagonally right uphill to the corner of the first field. Negotiate a stile of sorts and turn right to walk to the left of a wall. In summer the field edge is crammed with poppies and foxgloves. Bubnell Cliff Farm is but a short distance away to your left.

After 100 yards, where the wall corners away to the right, turn diagonally left to the far corner of a long field. Initially this is not in view but shortly a footpath finger post appears to guide you. Pass through the squeezer stile alongside the post onto the minor road linking Baslow with Hassop.

Turn right for 50 yards and then go left through another squeezer stile recognised by the presence of a footpath sign. When I surveyed the route

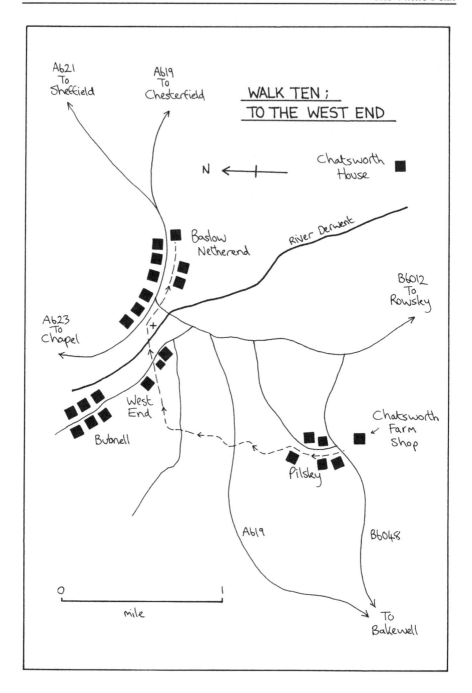

Ab21
To
Sheffield

Ab19
To
Chesterfield

WALK TEN ;
TO THE WEST END

N ←—

Chatsworth
House ■

River Derwent

Baslow
Netherend

Ab23
To
Chapel

B6012
To
Rowsley

West
End

Bubnell

Chatsworth
Farm
Shop

Pilsley

Ab19

B6048

0   1

mile

To
Bakewell

the path ran alongside a field of barley. After 100 yards, and by a wall corner, a T-junction is reached. Turn right, and with a wall on your left, advance to a stone step stile. The next field has an isolated stone barn in the middle so you could be forgiven for thinking that you had been transported suddenly into the heart of the Yorkshire Dales.

Continue a little to the right of a wall to a step stile adjacent to a gateway and then another by a five-barred gate. With Baslow church directly ahead as your marker, maintain direction to another stone step stile by a stone trough and a 'Private' sign. Beyond, a narrow path squeezes between a wall on your left and a hedge on your right until the Baslow to Bubnell road is reached. Cross directly onto the stone bridge to meet the A626.

Turn right, pass to the left of the parish church, pausing to inspect the clock face, and at the major roundabout go left in the direction signed to Sheffield and Chesterfield to your destination at the car park by Nether End.

11. Ancient Mythology

After an undulating start this route passes through a legendary and historic landscape.

Route: Birchover – The Portway – Harthill Moor – Youlgreave.

Start: The junction of Uppertown Lane with Main Street, Birchover. Map reference 239622. Altitude 248 metres.

Finish: Car park, Youlgreave. Map reference 206641. Altitude 200 metres.

Distance: 3½ miles.

Duration: 2 hours.

Map: The Peak District: White Peak Area, number 24 in the Ordnance Survey Outdoor Leisure series.

Public Transport: Birchover has several buses daily except Sunday from Bakewell and Matlock. In both towns there are connections to Sheffield, Derby, Chesterfield, Stockport, Buxton, Nottingham and Manchester.

Youlgreave has frequent buses to Bakewell daily except Sunday. Direct buses from Chesterfield, Sheffield, Bakewell and Buxton on summer Sundays and Bank Holidays.

By Car: Birchover may be reached by the minor road which leaves the B5056 near Eagle Tor at map reference 231627 or it may be approached by way of Stanton in Peak. There is restricted parking around the village.

For Youlgreave take the B5056 from the A6 at map reference 239658 and then the minor road signed to Alport and Youlgreave. An alternative approach is an unclassified road from the A5012, east of Newhaven at map reference 168603. There is a car park at the western end of Youlgreave village.

Refreshments: There are two pubs in Birchover and several in Youlgreave serving bar food.

Along the Way

Birchover

Birchover is one of the oldest settlements in the Peak District, receiving mention in Domesday Book as 'Barcovere' – a name derived from 'birch-covered slope'. The houses are constructed from the warm-looking pinkish sandstone to be found on nearby Stanton Moor. Their dates span three centuries but vernacular architecture changes so imperceptibly that these blend perfectly to provide a harmony to the village.

Amongst the oldest of these houses are the two village inns, the Red Lion and the Druid. The latter obtains its name from the druidical customs associated with Rowtor Rocks at the western end of the village. These are a gritstone outcrop of modest dimensions, weathered and eroded into a fantastic shape. Below the rocks is Rowtor Hall, which became the rectory and was home to the Reverend Thomas Eyre who had some rough stone seats made in the rocks so that he could sit there to admire the view. He was also responsible for the building of the tiny church, known as the Jesus Chapel, at the foot of the rocks. After his death in the early eighteenth century it was converted into a cheese warehouse but was restored to its original function in the nineteenth century.

A more recent vicar was responsible for carving the unique pulpit during the Second World War, when timber was extremely difficult to acquire. He is reputed to have used more than 20 varieties of wood, including some from the trees in his own garden. The pulpit is decorated with a rich and complex design based on animals and fish.

The Portway

The stretch of our route that runs its course between Cratcliff Rocks and Robin Hood's Stride is the Portway, a prehistoric route that ran through the Peak District from Mam Tor to Blackbrook near Ashbourne. It would be used not only by troops but by traders. It is probable that it had been in existence for hundreds, if not thousands, of years, before the Saxons gave it the name by which we know it today.

In Cratcliff Rocks is a cave once used by a religious hermit, as testified by the crucifix carved on the wall. Almost directly opposite, on the far side of the Portway, is Robin Hood's Stride, another rock outcrop with towers at either end. Legend would have us believe that Robin Hood cleared the gap between – about 20 yards. Their appearance from certain angles, however, gives the feature the shape of a gigantic house which has led to its other nickname, 'Mock Beggars Hall'.

A little further along is Harthill Moor Stone Circle, another prehistoric site. Today only four of the original nine stones survive. Alternative names are 'The Grey Ladies' or 'Nine Stones'. Numerous legends have developed around them, including one that on moonlit nights they twist and turn in a ritualistic dance. There are also stories of men leaning against one of them at night and finding clay pipes. When smoked, these apparently possessed hallucinogenic qualities, initiating the finder into a world of dancing fairies.

Yet another tradition relates that it was not Robin Hood who strode between the two pinnacles but a legendary Green Man. He stood with one foot on each of the towers while relieving himself. The sight of the water falling onto the meadow below petrified nine maidens who were dancing there.

On a more serious note, the Stone Circle may have been positioned in such a way that its alignment with the twin towers of Robin Hood's Stride allowed a study of the moon. In the days before sundials, clocks and other scientific timepieces, such knowledge would have been invaluable for local farmers and could also have been used in association with certain ancient religious ceremonies.

Only a few fields away, near present-day Harthill Moor Farm, is an Iron Age fort, erected no doubt to afford protection to travellers along the Portway.

Youlgreave

Continuing the mystical theme, it is said that every year on a certain November night the figures of a Roundhead and Cavalier can be seen locked together in fierce swordplay at Old Hall Farm. The room in which they materialise is known as the Duel Room.

On a more earthly level Youlgreave was mentioned in Domesday book as 'Giolgrove' and was one of the earliest lead-mining centres in the Peak District. The wealth generated by this and the market – its charter dated from 1340 – explain the grandeur of the parish church which is almost cathedral-like in its proportions. It projects onto the main road and is Norman in style with a square buttressed tower.

Otherwise one of the oldest buildings in the village is the Old Hall with its many mullioned windows dating from 1656. Even older is Old Hall Farm. One of the outstanding buildings is the Co-op, built in 1887 but now converted into a very popular youth hostel. Opposite is the Conduit Head or Fountain, built in 1829 to provide Youlgreave with its first piped water supply. To mark the improvement, well-dressing ceremonies were introduced and continue to this day.

Bradford Dale

The Route

Having first inspected the pinfolds by the start, walk westwards from the junction of Uppertown Road with Main Street to pass the Methodist Chapel before the road loses height slightly by the Red Lion Inn on your right. Some 100 yards further, before the road bends sharply to the right, continue forward along the lane which passes to the left of the Druid Inn and shortly afterwards passes the tiny church of St Michael and All Angels.

By the Old Vicarage the lane loses height and, near the drive entrance, meets an intersection. Stay straight ahead with a pond on your left as the countryside opens up views over Mires Farm to Manners Wood above Bakewell. After a further 200 yards the track takes a U-bend to the left; do not follow it round but keep forward towards a rusty five-barred gate within 10 yards and then veer left along a grassy path with a wall to your right.

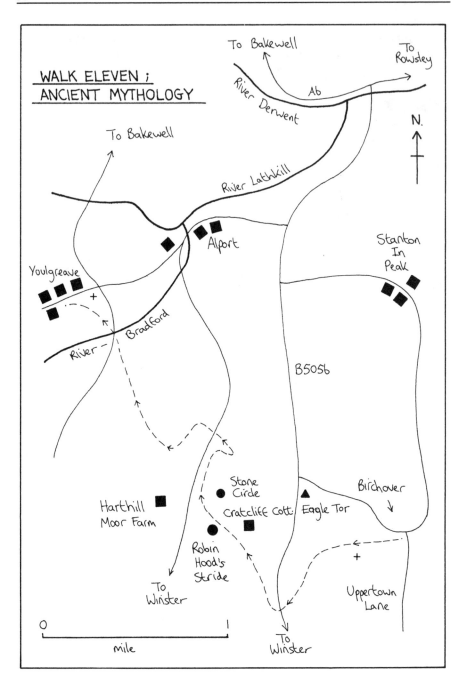

By now Eagle Tor, one of several rock outcrops in the vicinity, is to your right. On arriving at a Y-junction after approximately 70 yards, fork left for 12 yards to a stone step stile. Continue along the broad track as it forms a terrace along the contour, with a tree-covered slope on your left.

Pass an open barn and a derelict stone house alongside each other before meeting a Y-junction with four stone gateposts but no gate. Fork right along a narrower path which drops steeply to a footpath sign and a wooden stile allowing access to the B5056.

Turn left and walk for 100 yards before making a right turn into a narrow road. Cross a small stone bridge for another right turn over a wooden stile adjacent to a five-barred gate onto a path signed 'Cliff Lane ½ mile'. Further confirmation about your position may be gleaned from another notice announcing 'Private Drive. Footpath Only'.

As you climb rather gently you are treading the ancient Portway, used by our ancestors in the days long before Christ was born. It is a humbling yet exhilarating thought. Little wonder that this section of our walk passes through an area rich in myth and legend.

Through a gateway after about 300 yards, and by a footpath sign, fork left, away from another track leading to Cratcliff Rocks – although a diversion to the hermit's chapel is well rewarded.

From this point onwards the Portway narrows into a field path, climbing to another stile alongside a five-barred metal gate before continuing between two derelict stone walls. Robin Hood's Stride is only yards to the left; again, a diversion is in order.

Over the next stone step stile cross the ensuing field diagonally to the left while enjoying wide-ranging views over the plateau of the White Peak, including Lathkill Dale and Stanton Moor, identified by its TV transmitter.

On gaining the next stile, set in the field corner, maintain direction to a squeezer stile, accompanied by a five-barred gate and footpath sign. Exit onto the Elton–Alport road opposite Harthill Moor Farm. Notice the standing stone in the field to the right and the stone circle in the field beyond that.

Turn right along the road, which forms part of the route of the Limestone Way, a semi-long-distance route through the White Peak. As it starts to lose height it is partnered by elder trees and from nearby comes the unmistakable call of the pheasant.

On reaching a wood on the left the rate of descent quickens. A short distance before the road bends to the left, and by a wooden footpath finger post, turn left through a pair of stone gateposts to enter mixed woodlands. The path, wide and level initially, can be very muddy, especially after heavy rain.

Keep to the contour for a considerable distance, curving round leftwards to a wooden stile in the woodland boundary. Stay forward directly across the centre of the first field to a second stile by a footpath post. Turn right, following the Limestone Way sign, but soon curving round leftwards to a solitary gatepost and passing beneath overhead wires.

As it twists left the path begins its descent. By another gate post and the end of a wall turn right down the slope to a redundant stile. Pass either side and keep losing height to a further stile, also past its sell-by date.

At the foot of the slope stay to the left of a small gate, negotiate a wooden stile, cross Bleakley Dike and advance along a flagged path towards a small pylon. Keep this on your right in traversing a large field, with Youlgreave church as your target. Over the next stile, also by a five-barred gate, turn left to find a wall on your right before reaching a gateway. Turn right along an obvious path to a squeezer stile which is about five yards to the left of a five-barred gate.

Continue along the same line to a squeezer stile in the wall on your right, before crossing the field corner towards the right-hand end of a row of houses. Over the stile in front of these, turn right along the road, soon passing a stone barn to the right. Fifteen yards beyond that, by the next footpath sign, turn left through a squeezer stile onto a path which is accompanied by a low stone wall on the left. This leads to an attractive stone clapper bridge spanning the River Bradford, one of the clearest in the Peak District. At the far end turn left, negotiate yet another squeezer stile and walk the riverside path upstream.

After 100 yards, fork right up the short slope and, beyond a squeezer, continue along Holywell Lane to its junction with the main road through Youlgreave opposite the Old Hall. Turn left for the final 450 yards to the car park (less to the bus stop).

12. By Conksbury Bridge

Following field and riverside paths, this route links two attractive limestone villages while passing one of the most famous bridges of the Peak District.

Route: Over Haddon – Conksbury Bridge – River Lathkill – Alport.

Start: Car park, Over Haddon. Map reference 203664. Altitude 239 metres.

Finish: Alport village. Map reference 221645. Altitude 143 metres.

Distance: 2¼ miles.

Duration: 1½ hours.

Map: The Peak District: White Peak Area, number 24 in the Ordnance Survey Outdoor Leisure series.

Public Transport: There are frequent buses to both Over Haddon and Alport from Bakewell daily except Sunday.

Alport has buses from Sheffield, Bakewell and Buxton on summer Sundays and Bank Holidays.

By Car: Over Haddon may be approached by minor roads signed from Ashford (A6), Bakewell and Monyash. Car park in the village.

Alport is signed from the B5056 which leaves the A6 near Haddon Hall between Bakewell and Rowsley. There is a car park a few yards along the road to the right after the finish.

Refreshments: The Lathkill Hotel, Over Haddon, serves bar meals. The Yew Tree and other cafés in Over Haddon are open daily throughout the year.

Along the Way

Over Haddon

The village is attractively situated on a limestone shelf overlooking the River Lathkill with the result that it commands some superlative views. The 'Over' in its name formerly distinguished it from Nether Haddon which was demolished when Haddon Hall was built.

For centuries Over Haddon was closely associated with the lead-mining industry. There are still remains to be found in Lathkill Dale and the famous Magpie Mine is within easy walking distance. Sour Mill, dating from the sixteenth century, may still be seen near Lathkill Lodge (not on our route) although it is now used as a store.

The River Lathkill

Conksbury Bridge

This stands at a centuries-old crossing of the River Lathkill and was subsequently built to accommodate packhorses. The bridge also formed part of the Newhaven to Grindleford turnpike.

The Ordnance Survey map shows the site of a former medieval village on the west side of the river a little to the north of Conksbury Bridge. The name itself is of some interest because the second element is derived from the Old English 'Burh' meaning 'a fortified place'. Many such burghs or boroughs were erected in this region by King Alfred to keep the Danes at bay when the Danelaw was instituted. The first part, 'Conks', or 'Conkes' as it is sometimes spelled, means 'cranes', a bird little associated with the Lathkill these days. Perhaps it was interchangeable with 'herons'.

Raper Lodge

Quite close to Raper Lodge is another old packhorse bridge spanning the River Lathkill. It is known as Coalpit Bridge because the horses using it were transporting coal from the Chesterfield area. The bridge was also featured in the film, *The Virgin and the Gypsy*.

Alport

Its name meaning 'Old Market Town', Alport stands at the confluence of the Rivers Bradford and Lathkill and is one of the prettiest villages in the White Peak. For generations, strings of packhorses forded the river here until the present bridge was built in 1718. There has been a corn mill at Alport since at least Norman times when the then mill was valued at 5 shillings and 4 pence in Domesday Book. The present building, by the bridge, was still working to meet local needs until after the Second World War.

Two of the oldest buildings are Monks Hall and Lathkill House Farm, both from the seventeenth century. Like most other villages in this area Alport was actively involved in lead-mining.

The Route

Exit the car park in Over Haddon by turning right, but at the first junction, within a matter of yards, go left to follow the main street with its sturdy stone houses. One, in particular, has a very active dovecote. After a further 100 yards fork right into a narrower road which dips slightly before rising to pass to the right of the Lathkill Hotel.

A few yards beyond, where the road bends sharply leftwards, pass through a facing squeezer stile before veering through 45 degrees along a well-trodden field path. A little to your left is a most statuesque dead tree with a hole through its trunk. Negotiate a stone step stile followed at once by a traditional one alongside a finger post, which indicates your path to Conksbury and Lathkill Dale.

Along this section of the walk there is a good view of the hamlet of Conksbury on the far side of the River Lathkill and of Youlgreave, with its distinctive church, a little further away to the right. To add to your pleasure, the walking is first rate on a springy turf-path as it crosses the field.

Maintain direction to another traditional stile in a wire fence, while staying to the left of some hawthorns and well above Lathkill Dale. Pass between

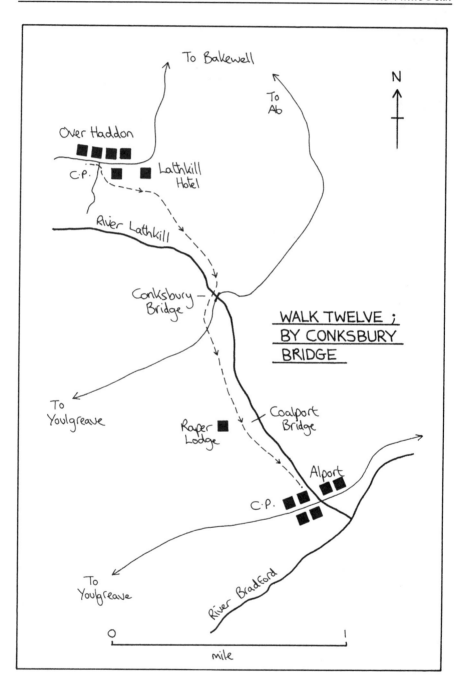

To Bakewell

To Ab

N

Over Haddon

C.P.

Lathkill Hotel

River Lathkill

Conksbury Bridge

To Youlgreave

Raper Lodge

Coalport Bridge

WALK TWELVE ;
BY CONKSBURY
BRIDGE

Alport

C.P.

To Youlgreave

River Bradford

0   1

mile

two wooden posts to a stile in another wire fence, followed by a through stile in a stone wall. At the subsequent Y-junction fork right and stay to the left of a wall. Descend gradually for the next 100 yards but, after passing through a small clump of trees, you descend more rapidly through two squeezer stiles to emerge onto a minor road. Turn right, still descending, to Conksbury Bridge which carries the Bakewell to Youlgreave road.

Cross the bridge, pausing to admire the view up the dale and also the enormous spread of butterbur by the river, before climbing for approximately 200 yards. A short distance from Conksbury Farm, and on a bend, turn left through a gate onto a wide track. There is no sign except for one forbidding cycling.

There is a wire fence on the left and a new plantation on the right. On this stretch the pheasant often offers greetings while, in season, bluebells and red campion add an extra dash of colour. In spring, it is also a good area for orange tip butterflies. Soon a wall closes in from the right and a through stile is reached after some 200 yards. Stay forward, descending to a squeezer stile by a five-barred gate before continuing a further 50 yards to another through stile beside a finger post.

Cross the bridleway which is signed to Haddon Hall. To your left is Coalpit Bridge while to your right is Raper Lodge. Notice, also to your left, the small green fishing house. Continue through a succession of lush riverside meadows, using the stiles as your guide, until finally emerging onto the main road through Alport close by the confluence of the Rivers Lathkill and Bradford.

13. Going to Town

This route takes you from one of the finest viewpoints in the White Peak to the home of that famous pudding.

Route: Monsal Head – Little Longstone – Monsal Trail – Bakewell station – Rutland Square.

Start: Monsal Head. Map reference 185715. Altitude 235 metres.

Finish: Rutland Square, Bakewell. Map reference 217685. Altitude 120 metres.

Distance: 4¼ miles.

Duration: 2½ hours.

Map: The Peak District: White Peak Area, number 24 in the Ordnance Survey Outdoor Leisure series.

Public Transport: Monsal Head is served by frequent daily (except Sunday) buses from Bakewell and Tideswell. On summer Sundays and Bank Holidays there are buses from Bakewell, Rochdale, Oldham, Ashton, Stalybridge and Glossop.

Bakewell has frequent daily buses from Manchester, Stockport, Buxton, Matlock, Derby, Nottingham, Chesterfield, Sheffield, Leek and Hanley. On summer Sundays and Bank Holidays there are buses from Rochdale, Oldham, Ashton, Stalybridge and Glossop.

By Car: Monsal Head is on the B6465 between the A623 at Wardlow Mires and the A6 at Ashford-in-the-Water. There is a large pay-and-display car park.

Bakewell is on the A6. It has large car parks but Mondays can be difficult because it is market day.

Refreshments: Monsal Head has a pub and cafés. Part way through the walk at Little Longstone there is a pub. Bakewell has a wide choice of pubs and cafés, and there is a coffee shop at the Country Bookstore by the former Hassop railway station.

Along the Way

Monsal Head

One of the most popular viewpoints in the Peak District, Monsal Head attracts thousands of visitors every year. There is a dramatic perspective of both the River Wye and the former Midland railway line, now the Monsal Trail.

The nearby village of Little Longstone has a long history of lead-mining and farming. The name of the village pub, the Packhorse is testimony to another aspect of its past history.

Bakewell

With a population in the region of 4,000, Bakewell is the largest place in the National Park. It has a history dating back to prehistoric times, signified by the existence of an Iron Age fort near Ballcross Farm (see Walk 9). There may have been a small Roman camp here, and it is believed that King Edward the Elder may have constructed a fortification on what is now known as Castle Hill.

In Norman times it was a royal manor held by William Peverel who built the castle at Castleton but subsequently it passed into the ownership of the Manners family. Its name means 'Badeca's Springs' and there were plans at one time to develop it as a spa town along the lines of Buxton.

The seventeenth-century Market Hall, now the Peak Park Information Centre and Tourist Office, is unusual in that it had windows rather than open arches. Bakewell maintains its long tradition and history as a trading centre with its large Monday cattle market.

The parish church, with its tall spire, overlooks the town and is dedicated to All Saints. It is believed to occupy the site of a Saxon church. Certainly the collection of stones inside the porch contains specimens of Saxon origin.

No mention of Bakewell would be complete without its pudding. Note that it is a pudding and not a tart. It originated by accident, being the result of a misunderstanding between the cook and her mistress at the Rutland Arms. Rather than including a mixture of eggs in the recipe, the cook poured it over the jam, much to the delight of the guests. Today visitors from all corners of the globe make a pilgrimage to the Old Original Bakewell Pudding Shop.

The Route

Before departing from Monsal Head, take a few minutes to absorb the view down into the steeply flanked dale, with the Wye flowing gently through

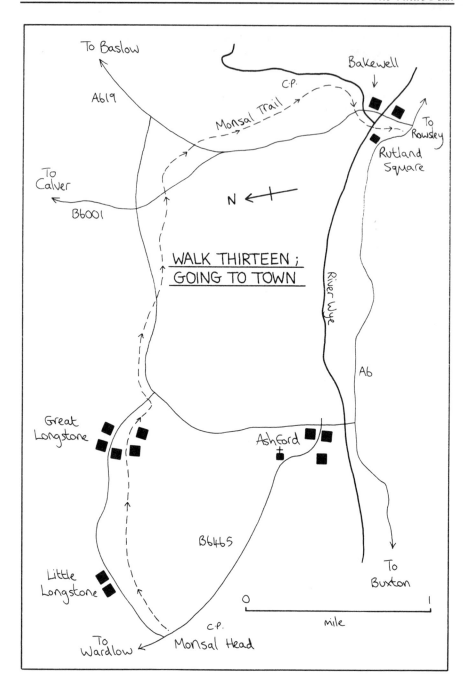

beneath an ancient clapper bridge at Upperdale and the former Midland Railway line thrusting along the contour from one tunnel to another.

With some reluctance, perhaps, turn your back on the Monsal Head Hotel to cross the B6465 into the facing road to Little and Great Longstone. On your left is the squat, stone-built Congregational Church of Little Longstone and, a few yards further but on the opposite side of the road, the ancient pinfold.

The village itself is a pleasing blend of attractive houses brightened by their colourful cottage gardens. Pass the Packhorse Inn; opposite the fine Manor House there is a small recess on the right, easy to recognise by its four five-barred gates. Turn right into this and take the stone step stile on the left for a path signed to Great Longstone. Ignore another stile with its sign to Ashford and the Monsal Trail.

In crossing the large field, aim slightly to the left of a solitary hawthorn and a small wired enclosure towards a clump of large trees on the crown of the rise. As you approach, keep these on your right to arrive at a wooden stile in a fence by the corner of a small plantation, which is the work of the Peak District National Park and the local landowner.

Advance 15 yards to a second stile before traversing the next field diagonally to the right for a squeezer stile, providing access to a lane. Cross this directly through a second squeezer, head over a very narrow field to a third and, continuing the same line of direction, go over a very large field to a fourth.

Staying close to the left-hand boundary hedge of a narrow field, keep forward to emerge onto a road in a housing estate in Great Longstone. Take the surfaced path opposite which runs between the houses to a sports field. Walk round the left-hand boundary of the cricket pitch and the adjacent football ground to a gateway in a facing wall.

Take the obvious road between bungalows until reaching Edge View Drive. Stay with this for about 150 yards. Beyond the last house turn left into a narrow path and, after 15 yards, make a right turn through a squeezer stile.

Using stiles as your guide, walk over two fields before following the very obvious and well-walked path as it curves gradually to the right across a large, green and lush pasture before descending easily to a stone step stile in a facing wall. Turn right for the short ascent of the embankment onto the Monsal Trail which has been constructed along the former Midland Railway line.

Turn left. Pass over a road junction below. The Trail itself is lined with bramble, thistle and trees where, in spring and early summer, the chattering of newborn birds may be heard. There is also an abundance of wild flowers including rosebay willowherb, red campion and bluebells.

The Monsal Trail passes over the B6001 Bakewell–Hassop road, where the Country Bookstore, housed in the former Hassop railway station, is well worth a browse and, if needed, a cup of coffee. Another road bridged is the A619 Bakewell–Baslow, with the unusually named Pineapple House adjacent.

On arriving at the former Bakewell station turn right off the Trail, go through the car park and turn left into Station Road. At the junction at the bottom of the hill make a left turn into Baslow Road, cross the fine old bridge spanning the River Wye, and walk by the National Park Information Centre and the Old Pudding Shop to reach Rutland Square.

14. By the Wye

Despite its popularity, the area through which this walk passes epitomises all that is so attractive about the White Peak. This makes an ideal walk for young children because it is short and has several places by the river suitable for picnics and even for supervised paddling.

Route: Monsal Head – Monsal Dale – Lees Bottom – White Lodge.

Start: Monsal Head. Map reference 185715. Altitude 235 metres.

Finish: White Lodge picnic area on the A6. Map reference 171705. Altitude 150 metres.

Distance: 1¾ miles.

Duration: 1 hour.

Map: The Peak District: White Peak Area, number 24 in the Ordnance Survey Outdoor Leisure series.

Public Transport: Monsal Head is served by frequent daily (except Sunday) buses from Bakewell and Tideswell. On summer Sundays and Bank Holidays there are buses from Bakewell, Rochdale, Oldham, Ashton, Stalybridge and Glossop.

White Lodge has frequent daily buses from Manchester, Stockport, Buxton, Bakewell, Matlock, Derby, Nottingham, Leek, and Hanley.

By Car: Monsal Head is on the B6465 between the A623 at Wardlow Mires and the A6 at Ashford-in-the-Water. There is a large pay-and-display car park. White Lodge car park is adjacent to the south side of the A6 from which it is signed.

Refreshments: Pub serving bar meals and cafés at Monsal Head.

Along the Way

Monsal Head

See Walk 13.

The River Wye

One of the major rivers of the Peak District, this rises on the moors above Buxton and flows through Poole's Cavern to emerge in Spring Gardens, before continuing through Wyedale, Miller's Dale, Monsal Dale and Bakewell to join the River Derwent at Rowsley.

River Wye, near Ashford

The Route

From the B6465 walk along the north side of the Monsal Head Hotel and to the south of the short stay car park. The road is signed to Cressbrook. After the first 50 yards, where the road bends acutely to the right by Monsal View café, pass through a facing squeezer stile in the wall.

Take time to study the signs, because several paths start from this point. Go down a flight of three steps and after a very short distance turn left to a stile. Initially the path descends gradually, through what appears to be natural broad-leaved woodland, with a fence on your right, before levelling out to work its course along the contour. The ground slopes steeply to left and right

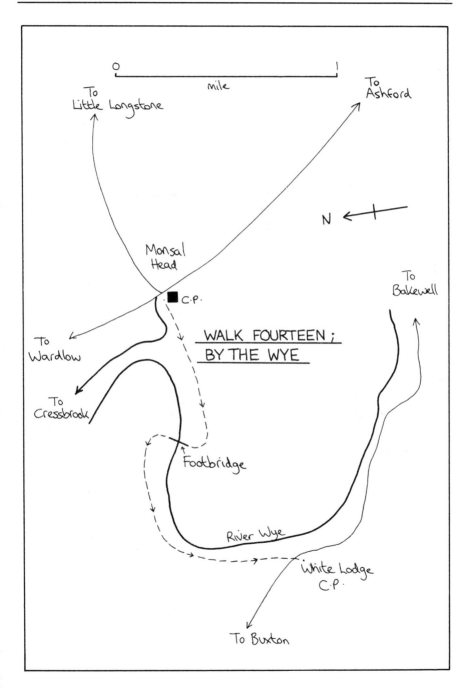

To Little Longstone

To Ashford

mile

N

Monsal Head

C.P.

To Bakewell

WALK FOURTEEN ; BY THE WYE

To Wardlow

To Cressbrook

Footbridge

River Wye

White Lodge C.P.

To Buxton

and it is covered with red campion, bramble and wild roses, not to mention an abundance of cuckoo spit deposited by the tiny froghopper.

When the fence on the right ends you start to descend quickly, with the sound of the River Wye growing louder at every step. Notice the occasional dead tree hereabouts pockmarked with woodpecker holes, covered with fungus, or perhaps both. In spring these woods resound with the songs of chiffchaff, willow warbler, blackbird, wren, robin, thrush, blue tit, great tit and chaffinch.

Eventually emerge onto the bank of the Wye by a substantial weir, over which the water cascades at great speed. A few yards beyond turn right over the river by means of a blue metal footbridge. At the far end turn left to follow the Wye downstream along a broad path. This widens as the valley opens up slightly with its steep, thickly wooded slopes under Brushfield Hough. The river, occasionally placid, occasionally tumbling over mini rapids, is graced with mallard and moorhen, its banks enlivened from time to time by clumps of marsh marigold.

On reaching a four-armed finger post continue in the same direction which is signed to White Lodge. Taddington Dale and Brushfield are for days when we want a stiff climb. Within 20 yards of the signs, negotiate a ladder stile to cross Lees Bottoms, a slightly sloping meadow, to a small flight of stone steps and a squeezer stile.

Turn left along the A6 for the bus stop to Bakewell. Cross more or less directly for the car park. If travelling towards Buxton and beyond, turn right to walk just over 100 yards to a lay-by on the south side of the road, where you will see the bus stop sign.

15. Through Wooded Dale

A walk which takes you through delightful woodland and along the valley of the River Wye.

Route: Sheldon – Little Shacklow Wood – Wyedale – Ashford-in-the-Water.

Start: Sheldon. Map reference 175688. Altitude 302 metres.

Finish: Ashford-in-the-Water. Map reference 195697. Altitude 138 metres.

Distance: 2 miles.

Duration: 1 hour.

Map: The Peak District: White Peak Area, number 24 in the Ordnance Survey Outdoor Leisure series.

Public Transport: Sheldon has buses from Bakewell on Mondays only.

Ashford-in-the-Water has frequent daily buses from Manchester, Stockport, Buxton, Hanley, Leek, Bakewell, Matlock, Derby, Nottingham and Sheffield. There are buses from Tideswell daily except Sunday. On summer Sundays and Bank Holidays there are buses from Rochdale, Oldham, Ashton, Stalybridge, Glossop, Macclesfield and Chesterfield.

By Car: Sheldon may be approached by a minor road (signed) leaving the A6 at map reference 193685 or from the A515 by minor roads through Monyash. Roadside parking only.

Ashford is adjacent to the A6 and is well signed from the bypass. There is limited parking opposite the church and by the Sheepwash Bridge.

Refreshments: There are cafés and pubs serving bar meals in Ashford.

Along the Way

Sheldon

Unfortunately Sheldon is too often associated only with the celebrated Magpie Mine so that other aspects of this charming village are neglected. It consists of little more than a half mile stretch of road flanked by houses but gains an added attractiveness from the broad grass swathes which separate them from the road.

As with so many White Peak villages it receives a mention in Domesday Book, as 'Scheldaun', but the story of human activity in this area goes back to at least 6,000BC. A rock shelter, paved with limestone slabs and dating from the Middle Stone Age, has been excavated to yield scores of artefacts. It is surmised that its occupants were involved in quarrying in the vicinity.

400 years ago Sheldon presented a completely different appearance. To the north of the village was a large field of 170 acres known as the Common, a piece of land subsequently divided by stone walls. In recent centuries there have been fluctuations in population reflecting the ups and downs of the lead-mining industry. During a period of expansion in the eighteenth century there was an influx of Cornish miners.

The present church is comparatively modern. Built in the nineteenth century, it replaced a former chapel-of-ease dating from the fifteenth century.

Sheldon has one unusual claim to fame. In the seventeenth century a duck was reported as flying up into a tree and then disappearing from sight. When the tree was cut down and sawn into sections the outline of a duck was found. This, it is alleged, is the origin of the word 'duckboards'. Perhaps you need a pinch of salt when visiting Sheldon.

Ashford-in-the-Water

Every year thousands of visitors flock into the village to see the Sheepwash Bridge spanning the River Wye where, in days gone by, all local sheep were dipped prior to shearing. This practice is still maintained, but only as a tourist attraction on certain days of the year. The Sheepwash Bridge occupies the site of a former ford which provided a vital link in the trans-Peak route known as the Portway, which existed in prehistoric times (see Walk 11). Its continuation now forms part of the road leading to Monsal Head.

The village name is of Saxon origin and it is not difficult to work out that it means 'The Ash by the Ford'. Athelstan, grandson of Alfred the Great and the first king of all England, granted a charter to Ashford which was then the only village between Buxton and Bakewell. Its proximity to Sheldon and the presence of chert makes it likely that people lived here in prehistoric times to exploit the mineral deposits. Again, in common with other villages in this area it was associated with lead-mining and as early as 1066 it contributed 50 slabs of lead to the Royal Treasury; it had its own Barmote

Court to regulate the local industry. 'Black Marble' was also extracted from quarries between Ashford and Sheldon: large amounts were used for interior decorations at Chatsworth and the floor of the sanctuary in the parish church of Holy Trinity is paved with it.

The present site has probably been occupied by a church since before the Norman Conquest. There was definitely one there by 1200, parts of which survived a drastic rebuilding in the last century. Inside the church are several 'Maidens' Crants', which were garlands placed on the coffins of unmarried girls until the practice ceased early in the nineteenth century.

Ashford: the sheepwash bridge

The Route

From the telephone kiosk in the centre of Sheldon village walk along the road in an easterly direction, diverting along a bridleway on your left to have a look at the unusual church of St Michael and All Angels with its rounded eastern end and splendid roof of many narrow beams. Afterwards return to the road where a left turn will soon carry you beyond the last of the houses.

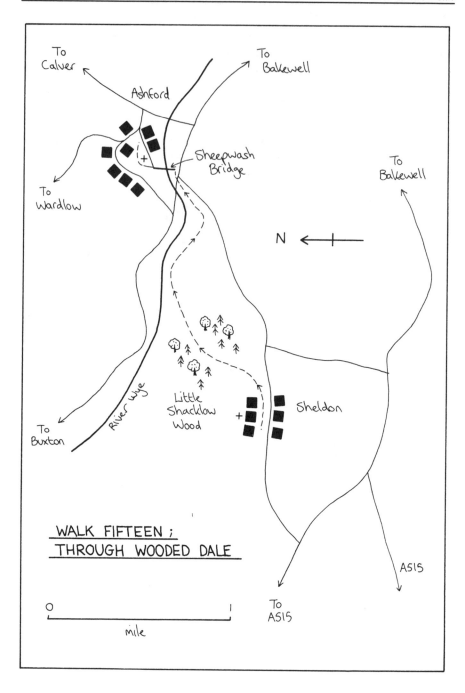

To
Calver

To
Bakewell

Ashford

Sheepwash
Bridge

To
Bakewell

To
Wardlow

N ←—

River Wye

Little
Shacklow
Wood

Sheldon

To
Buxton

WALK FIFTEEN ;
THROUGH WOODED DALE

0   1
mile

To
A515

A515

A little way after the traffic de-restriction signs the road dips steeply to a very sharp bend by which, on your left, stands Lower Farm with its extremely attractive garden – a mass of flowers in high summer.

By the far boundary wall of the farm, immediately round the bend, turn left over a stone step stile with a finger post alongside. The footpath runs a couple of feet to the right of a broad track as it embarks on a gradual descent into the valley. After 100 yards stay to the right of a facing wall corner to a junction. Fork left, keeping to the right of a drystone wall forming part of a sewage plant enclosure. After a further 100 yards negotiate a wooden stile to enter Little Shacklow Wood.

The next section of the walk is the highlight of the route, a stretch to be savoured at a leisurely pace to absorb the birdsong and admire the rich profusion of flora. The trees are mixed deciduous including oak, ash, elder and rowan. There is a dense undergrowth of nettles, bracken, dock and thistle. Even the slightest of breezes will cause a rustling of leaves. The flora include buttercup, celandine, red campion, wild garlic, viper's bugloss and purple loosestrife. The rich symphony of birdsong is provided by thrush, blackbird, blue tit, great tit, wren, jay, magpie, green woodpecker and chaffinch.

The path descends, sometimes gradually, sometimes more sharply. It can be muddy and, in sections, is quite stony but not excessively so. Lower down the clough the flanks steepen and there is the occasional small outcrop of limestone.

Eventually the path emerges into a small clearing overgrown with nettles. At this point it appears to be about to meet a T-junction but in fact merely turns through 90 degrees to the right as it develops into a wider track, still losing altitude but not at the same rate, until it reaches a wooden stile adjacent to a wooden five-barred gate. Over this stay to the left of a stone wall with more open and less wooded land on your left. In time the busy A6 comes into view some distance ahead with a high green ridge behind it.

After approximately 350 yards a T-junction is reached with the corner of Little Shacklow Wood on the right and immediately in front of a derelict stone wall. Turn right through a gateway with a stile alongside to be guided by a yellow waymark bearing the numeral 3. The path is now good and firm with the River Wye meandering on your left. The scene would be perfect except for the blight of traffic noise from the A6, contrasting with the peace and quiet of the woodland section of this walk.

After a considerable distance by the river climb a ladder stile alongside a five-barred gate to walk an extra 50 yards to the narrow road linking the A6 with Sheldon. Exercising extreme caution turn left along this for 300 yards to meet the A6. Turn right in the direction of Bakewell and use the pavement on the south side of the road.

After approximately 250 yards, and just before the very prominent direction sign, cross the road and then make a left turn over Sheepwash Bridge. At the far end turn right for the remaining few yards to Ashford church and the bus stop.

16. Down Deep Dale

This route follows field paths and bridleways before dropping down one of the many dry dales in the White Peak.

The Route: Monyash – High Low – Deep Dale – White Lodge.

Start: The village green, Monyash. Map reference 150666. Altitude 263 metres.

Finish: White Lodge car park and picnic site. Map reference 171705. Altitude 150 metres.

Distance: 3½ miles.

Duration: 2 hours.

Map: The Peak District: White Peak Area, number 24 in the Ordnance Survey Outdoor Leisure series.

Public Transport: Monyash has daily (except Sunday) buses from Buxton. On Mondays there are services from Bakewell, Leek and Hartington.

White Lodge is served by daily buses from Manchester, Stockport, Buxton, Bakewell, Matlock, Derby, Nottingham, Hanley and Leek.

By Car: Monyash lies on the B5055 which runs from Bakewell to the A515 at map reference 132659. It is signed from both ends. It may also be approached from the A6 through Taddington using a series of minor roads. There is a car park in the village.

White Lodge car park is adjacent to and signed from the A6 west of Ashford-in-the-Water.

Refreshments: Pub serving bar meals and cafés in Monyash. At the finish the nearest refreshments are at Ashford-in-the-Water (approximately 1½ miles).

Along the Way

Monyash

This is a popular starting point for walkers heading towards Lathkill Dale, although our walk takes us in a completely different direction. It is one of the highest villages on the limestone plateau. Standing on a bed of clay, it has always enjoyed a good water supply with more than 20 springs supplying five meres, of which only one now remains near the village centre. Close by is the well that is dressed during the annual festival.

Market Cross, Monyash

There is little to suggest prehistoric settlement in the area but the village was mentioned in Domesday Book. Its name is believed to mean 'Many Ash'. During the fourteenth century it was granted a market charter as testified by the medieval market cross which still stands by the centre of the village. Markets were held weekly and there was a much larger fair twice a year. Today the market has disappeared except for the modern revival held on the Spring and August Bank Holiday Mondays.

Parts of the chancel and tower of the twelfth-century church, dedicated to St Leonard, are incorporated into the present building, which mainly dates from the nineteenth century. The font is fifteenth-century and the oak vestment chest even older. One of the former vicars of Monyash fell to his death from what is known as Parson Tor near Ricklow Quarry, once a source of Ashford marble (see Walk 15).

Monyash shares with Hawes in the Yorkshire Dales the distinction of having been an important centre for the Society of Friends. In the Derbyshire instance it resulted from an eighteenth-century immigration of miners from other parts of the country to work for the London Lead Company. There was a tiny Quaker meeting house, still to be seen near the present Methodist Church, and a burial ground for use by members of the Society of Friends.

Even the most casual glance at the map with its scatterings of abandoned mine shafts will reveal that Monyash was once an important centre for lead-mining. Because of frequent disputes and attempts to evade the payment of dues, tolls and taxes, a Barmote Court was established to govern the industry, with powers to enforce strictly any laws it made.

Our walk passes close to **Magpie Mine**, which is now the best preserved lead mine in the country. Lead was worked there from as early as 1740 but the mine did not become profitable until 1810 when, in one four-month period, it produced ore valued at £2,088. Between 1868 and 1870 that figure rose to £19,000. Flooding was a serious problem throughout its working life and considerable sums of money were invested to enable work to proceed. There were also disputes with neighbouring mines which developed seriously in 1833 when three miners were killed by smoke from the Redsoil Mine. Seventeen men were charged with murder but all were acquitted.

Not surprisingly agriculture, especially sheep grazing, has always played a vital role in the economy of the village as shown by the pinfold to be found along the early part of our route. Monyash has also in its time produced candles and ropes, two items vital for use in the lead mines.

The Route

Reluctantly tearing yourself away from the attractive green in the heart of Monyash, head northwards along Chapel Lane, the minor road signed to Flagg and Sheldon, soon passing to the left of the Methodist chapel which gives the street its name. After approximately 250 yards turn right into another minor road signed to Sheldon but, within 20 yards, go left over a stone step stile, easily recognised by the wooden footpath finger post alongside.

Stay just to the left of the wall while climbing gently to a second stile in a facing wall. Continue with the original wall on your right across several fields, guided by the stiles – there are two large TV dishes away to your left. In early summer, a glorious spread of yellow is created by the prolific buttercups in the meadows.

On clear days there is an extensive vista across the plateau of the White Peak, the green fields delineated and patterned by miles of drystone walls. Between stiles four and five you will pass a wooden stile abutting the wall on your right which has no apparent purpose.

On approaching a farm to your right there are some stone drinking troughs set into the wall, which has been your constant companion since leaving the road. Over the next stone step stile curve to the right, still clinging to the left of the wall – which houses more stone drinking troughs – and staying outside the farmhouse boundary, to reach another stile.

Divert diagonally right over the corner of the next field for 50 yards to a stile which not only boasts a finger post close by but also a round red disc secured to a pole, a sure and certain waymarker and guide.

Turn right and aim for a second red disc before staying forward to a stone step stile set into a wooden frame. Maintain this new line of direction – now with a wall on your immediate left – while traversing a field dominated by ox-eye daisies and clover to a stile. Keep the wall on your left in passing several grassed-over spoil heaps, evidence of former lead mines in the vicinity, and with Hard Rake Plantations away to your right. This name alone is another indicator of the former industrial activity hereabouts.

Over the next stile stick to the right of the wall to yet another stile followed, after a mere six yards, by a wooden stile adjacent to a five-barred gate.

This allows entry to a walled lane which passes beneath some overhead

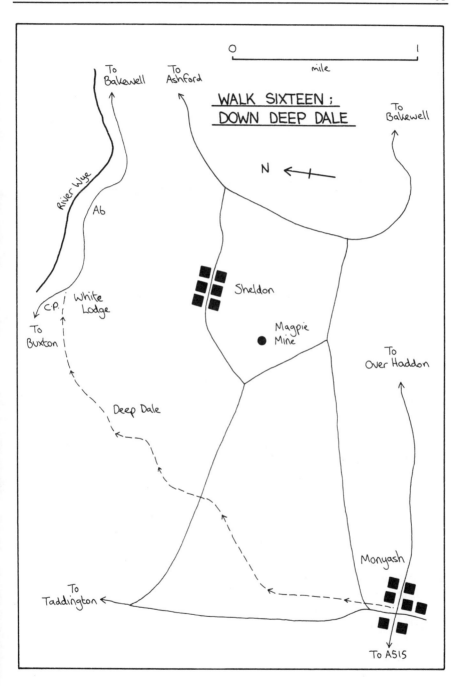

WALK SIXTEEN;
DOWN DEEP DALE

power lines; in summer, the skylark serenades with its continuous trilling and the wheatear hops and flies along the coping stones.

The lane is fringed with umbellifers, bramble, purple loosestrife, docks and nettles. There is a distant view of Flagg village to the left, while in the medium distance to the right are the unmistakable remains of the Magpie Mine. At this point, too, the lane passes close to High Low, a prehistoric burial ground distinguished by the solitary hawthorn on its crown.

Eventually this lane emerges onto the road from Bakewell to Chelmorton. To the left is a large lay-by which could be used by anyone wishing to shorten this walk (map reference 158685).

Cross the road directly into a wide, walled lane signposted 'A Bridle Road Through Deep Dale for Taddington Dale'. It is lined with butterbur, thistles, eyebright and forget-me-nots as its descends gradually. In the valley bottom, where the lane curves leftwards for its climb towards Taddington, look out for a seven-barred metal gate in the wall on your right. There, turn right through a stile on the left-hand side of this gate, which is identified by a minute yellow waymarker arrow.

Proceed down Deep Dale, staying close in to the left of a wall. On reaching a public bridleway sign turn right through a small gate and then immediately left so that the line of direction is maintained, but now to the right of the wall. Look high to your left for a view of Deep Dale Lodge, apparently perched very precariously high on the valley flank.

Gradually the sloping valley sides acquire a covering of hawthorn and elder and, as the descent continues gradually, these are replaced by more dense woodland which echoes to the songs of scores of birds.

Well down the valley where a small rock outcrop emerges, curve round to the right towards a Y-junction complete with finger post. Fork left in accordance with the sign to White Lodge. The descent steepens appreciably as you walk under a bower of wild roses to a stone step stile. Turn right, cross a succession of limestone slabs embedded in the ground and meander through trees to a stile. Drop the final 20 yards to the car park at White Lodge. If you are travelling by bus proceed through the car park to the A6. For those heading in the direction of Buxton, the stop is in a lay-by some 250 yards west of the exit. The stop for buses travelling towards Bakewell is also west of the car park entrance but much closer.

17. Another Deep Dale

Opening as a gentle stroll along lanes followed by field paths, this walk evolves into a gentle descent along a rocky path.

Route: Chelmorton – Shepley Farm – Deep Dale – Topley Pike – Wyedale.

Start: Chelmorton church. Map reference 114703. Altitude 382 metres.

Finish: Wyedale car park. Map reference 103725. Altitude 241 metres.

Distance: 3 miles.

Duration: 1½ hours.

Map: The Peak District: White Peak Area, number 24 in the Ordnance Survey Outdoor Leisure series.

Public Transport: Chelmorton is served by buses from Buxton daily except Sunday.

Wyedale car park is served by daily buses from Manchester, Stockport, Buxton, Bakewell, Derby, Nottingham, Leek and Hanley.

By Car: From Buxton drive south along the A515 in the direction of Ashbourne. At Brierlow Bar fork left onto the A5270. By Far Ditch Farm fork right onto a minor road signed to Chelmorton and shortly afterwards turn left for the village centre and church. Alternatively it may be reached via a minor road (signed) which leaves the A515 near Pomeroy (map reference 114677). Limited parking near the church.

Wyedale car park is signed from the A6 at Topley Pike, approximately 3 miles east of Buxton.

Refreshments: The Church Inn, Chelmorton, serves bar meals.

Along the Way

Chelmorton

The church of St John the Baptist enjoys the distinction of being the highest in the Diocese of Derby. Chelmorton now forms part of a united parish with Monyash and Taddington but it had its own vicar until 1950, as had been the custom since at least the thirteenth century when the church was built.

Several portions of this original building still survive including the chancel arch, the octagonal pillars, the piscina, sedilia and the lower windows in the side aisles. The upper windows, far more elaborate, are younger by two centuries, installed when the height of the walls was raised. The unusual stone screen, separating choir from nave, was carved a few years prior to the Black Death. The porch and doorway form the newest part of the building, dating from the reign of Elizabeth I. The weather vane is another rarity in that it takes the form of a locust, an insect closely associated with St John.

Chelmorton church

Chelmorton is a linear village, its position dictated by the 'Illy Willy Water', the stream which emerges from Chelmorton Low. Most of the farms are along this street, with their medieval crofts – now enclosed by drystone walls – behind them. This preservation of the old farming system is considered to be the finest example of its kind in England and the National Park is following a conservation policy.

The surrounding plateau is peppered with disused mine shafts while quarrying, either for limestone or basalt, has long featured in the economy of the village. In view of its proximity to Arbor Low, it is not surprising that there are prehistoric associations in the form of burial mounds on Chelmorton Low.

The Route

From the Church Inn at Chelmorton walk down the hill for a few yards to the road junction and, by the footpath finger post, turn right into Old Coalpit Lane, a name indicative of ancient use. For the first few yards it is lined with houses before emerging into open country to provide a good view of the field enclosure system. To the right is Chelmorton Low.

By Shepley Farm stay forward through a five-barred gate and, after a further 250 yards, through a second. In early summer the flanking fields are carpeted with flowers and there are extensive views over much of the White Peak plateau, marred only by the presence of quarries in the distance at Earl Sterndale.

Pass over a cattle grid to reach the A5270. Turn left and, after a few paces, go right into a walled lane which loses height gradually. Eschew the first lane leading off to the left but, where your lane curves round to the right, shortly before a dilapidated barn and some sheep pens, turn left into another lane.

After approximately 70 yards turn right over a stone step stile before crossing a narrow field to a second stile in the facing wall. Continue diagonally left to a third stile in another facing wall, taking your line of direction from a conspicuous house standing in front of a wood on the opposite side of the valley.

Maintain the same line of advance over the third field while passing a little to the right of a telegraph pole. Over the next stone step stile swing sharply left to a wooden stile in a wall and a wire fence which forms the lower boundary of the field. The stile is about 20 yards to the right of the field corner.

Corkscrew down the steep, almost vertical, side of the valley to the floor of Deep Dale. Five yards before a wooden stile in the facing wire fence there is a not very obvious intersection of paths. Turn right onto the one which runs behind a large tree and to the right of the fence before crossing the bottom of a scree slope rising to your right.

At this point the path is not very clear so careful navigation is needed. The valley bottom is lush with vegetation, there being an abundance of red

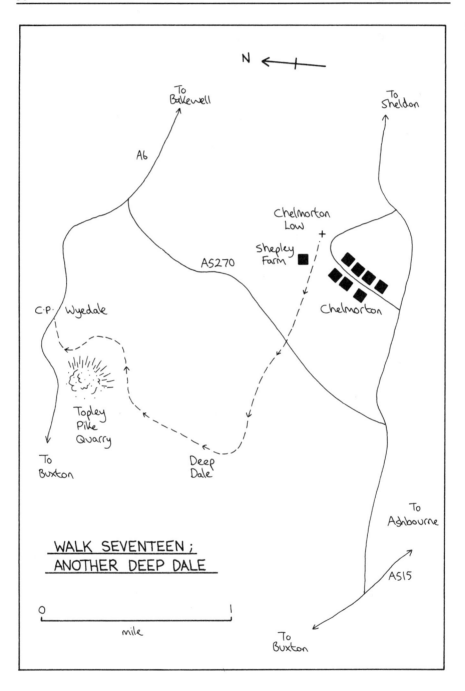

N ← +

To
Bakewell

A6

To
Sheldon

Chelmorton
Low

A5270

Shepley
Farm ■

Chelmorton

C.P. Wyedale

Topley
Pike
Quarry

To
Buxton

Deep
Dale

To
Ashbourne

WALK SEVENTEEN ;
ANOTHER DEEP DALE

A515

0   1

mile

To
Buxton

campion, rosebay willowherb and trees. Lose height gradually while placing your feet with care – the ground is littered with embedded rocks and stones some of which are obscured by the long grass and other plants.

After a considerable distance, and by a concrete bunker on your left accompanied by a notice about blasting times to your right, the narrow path suddenly develops into a broad track, separated on the left from a limestone lagoon by a wire fence and 'Keep Out' signs. This is one occasion when you will not wish to trespass.

Later the track narrows again while the downward gradient steepens. The buildings of Topley Pike Quarry come into view. As the path levels it reaches a T-junction. Turn left, so walking to the right of a fence. Where the path meets the approach road to the quarry make a right turn for the final 200 yards of descent to the A6. The National Park's Wyedale car park is directly opposite while the bus stop is to the left.

18. Priests and Millers

Initially a level route along field paths followed by a dramatic descent.

Route: Taddington – Horse Stead – Priestcliffe – Miller's Dale.

Start: Taddington village. Map reference 141711. Altitude 358 metres.

Finish: The church, Miller's Dale. Map reference 141733. Altitude 220 metres.

Distance: 2½ miles.

Duration: 1½ hours.

Map: The Peak District: White Peak Area, number 24 in the Ordnance Survey Outdoor Leisure series.

Public Transport: Taddington has daily bus services from Nottingham, Derby, Matlock, Bakewell, Buxton, Stockport, Manchester, Leek and Hanley.

Miller's Dale has daily bus services from Buxton, Tideswell, Sheffield and Chesterfield. On summer Sundays and Bank Holidays there are buses from Barnsley, Castleton, Mansfield, Derby, Bakewell and Ashbourne.

By Car: Taddington is bypassed by the A6 from which it is signed east of Buxton. Roadside parking only. Miller's Dale is approached by the B6049 which runs from the A623 at Tideswell Moor to the A6 near Taddington. There is a National Park car park on the site of the former railway station.

Refreshments: Bar meals are available at the Angler's Rest Inn – about 100 yards down the road signed to Litton Mill at the finish of the walk – and at the Queen's Arms Inn in Taddington village at the start. There is a café opposite the car park at Miller's Dale.

Along the Way

Taddington

Taddington has a long history dating back into prehistoric times. At Five Wells (not on our route) two burial chambers have been excavated to reveal several bodies, along with artefacts including flint tools. There is some evidence to suggest the presence of a wattle and daub church long before the Norman Conquest, and the cross in the churchyard is certainly of Saxon origin.

Not surprisingly the village receives a mention in Domesday Book although there is no reference to a church. The present building, sited in a large churchyard with a commanding perspective over the surrounding country-side, was constructed in 1373 when the Duchy of Lancaster ordered that three oak trees be felled for the roof timbers, which may still be seen. It is dedicated to St Michael and All Angels and contains some very old items of interest such as two stone fonts, one of which spent many years in a local pub being used for the washing of beer glasses!

If we are to believe everything written on the gravestones, Taddington must be one of the healthiest spots in Britain: for William Hexed is recorded as being 218 years old when he was laid to rest there.

Taddington Hall, built during the eighteenth century, is reputedly haunted as the result of a murder following a family quarrel.

Taddington: to be avoided?

Priestcliffe

This tiny hamlet overlooking Miller's Dale has examples of 'lynches' or broad terraces typical of the Anglo-Saxon method of agriculture. The first part of the name suggests ecclesiastical associations while the second half is usually interpreted to mean 'precipice' or 'steep slope', either of which would fit the topography of Priestcliffe.

Miller's Dale

See Walk 7.

The Route

From the road junction part way along Taddington's main street walk eastwards in the direction of Bakewell, before turning left through the lych-gate and taking the surfaced path by the west end of the parish church of St Michael and All Angels. Where this terminates by the church porch, continue forward along the green path leading to a gated through stile. Advance immediately to the right of a drystone wall.

Follow this as it curves round to the right until a stone step stile provides an exit onto the A6. Cross directly before turning right for 20 yards along the wide grass verge and turning left over an unsigned stone step stile at the western end of a small lay-by: this is difficult to see but has a wooden pylon behind it.

Turn right at once along an overgrown walled lane heading in the direction of Horse Stead. After 100 yards and where the lane appears to peter out, swing to the left and walk to the right of a wall. In the far corner of the field, as walls converge and the lane recommences, turn left through a squeezer stile which boasts rough wooden uprights to supplement a single stone one.

Cross the field corner for some 50 yards to another squeezer stile. Advance initially for eight yards with a wall on your left and then keep to the right of some oak trees before dropping gradually towards a large single oak in the centre of the field. Beyond this, stay to the right of a wall as the path makes its way through a shallow valley, carpeted in summer with buttercups, daisies and forget-me-nots. Pass through a small collection of trees and then a wall gap (while still remaining to the right of the wall) to reach a squeezer stile in a wall corner.

Now, to the left of a wall which is almost totally obscured by hawthorn and elder, continue forward across a small field to a through stile; from here the right-hand corner of a barn becomes your guiding beacon. The next through stile, waymarked with yellow paint, provides access to a lane. Ignore a facing stile, also waymarked, choosing rather to make a right turn along the lane to a T-junction within 200 yards.

Turn left into another lane. After 50 yards and by a finger post to Miller's

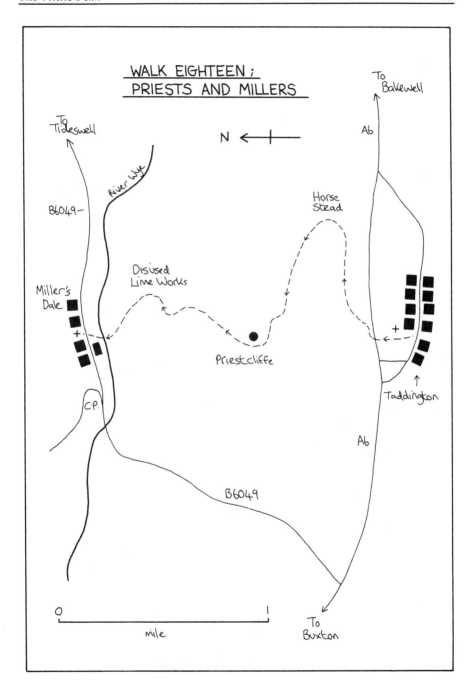

WALK EIGHTEEN ;
PRIESTS AND MILLERS

To Bakewell

To Tideswell

River Wye

N ←——|—→

A6

B6049—

Horse Stead

Disused Lime Works

Miller's Dale

Priestcliffe

Taddington

C.P.

A6

B6049

0 ————————————— 1
mile

To Buxton

Dale, make an acute turn to the left onto a narrow path which climbs some 20 yards to a stile. Continue forward between a wall on your left and a bank on your right, both of which are partially concealed by umbellifers and nettles.

Climb gently for 100 yards to the minuscule hamlet of Priestcliffe and a stile by Stopes Cottage, a charming rose-covered house on your right. At the T-junction after a further five yards turn left to another junction within 10 yards. Take the second track on the right signed to Miller's Dale. Pass a roofless building on your left, somewhat incongruously advertised as an MOT Test Centre. After 100 yards along this lane turn right over a stone step stile alongside another finger post pointing to Miller's Dale.

Head diagonally left to a through stile set into the wall on your left about 100 yards from the near wall corner. Cross the centre of the next field to a stile directly opposite before maintaining direction over a third field to another stile. Traverse the ensuing field by following the path as it heads towards a wall on your right and a squeezer stile set into the corner of a wall.

From there stay to the right of a wall while dropping very gradually into another broad, shallow valley carpeted with grass and clover and where the skylark mixes its flute-like song with the more strident calls of the jackdaw. As the path starts to climb go over a stone step stile on your left but maintain direction with the wall now on your right.

The next stone step stile is set in a wall corner; after this stay to the right of a wall to a squeezer stile in a facing wall. Continue forward over the centre of the next field to yet another squeezer, from where there is a splendid view of Tideswell church, the 'cathedral of the Peak', in the far distance. Closer to hand there is a fenced-off mine shaft to your right.

Beyond the stile turn right to pass between a wire fence on your left and a wall on your right. After 20 yards follow the path as it swings round to the left, moving away from the wall and staying close to the fence.

From this point onwards the path drops precipitately while skirting the fenced boundary of an enormous abandoned quarry which, because of its wide selection of flora including field scabious, eyebright, leadwort and dark mullein, is now a nature reserve owned by the Derbyshire Wildlife Trust. The railing on your left is an extremely useful aid during the descent.

By the quarry floor curve diagonally right as you head, still downwards, towards a wood resonant with birdsong in spring and early summer. Pass through the wood and large expanses of butterbur with its rhubarb-like leaves to a small flight of stone steps before crossing a small footbridge, which is almost completely overgrown by lush vegetation.

Negotiate a squeezer stile onto the Monsal Trail (see Walk 13) and cross onto the narrow path which turns towards the left as it loses height to the River Wye. Turn right over the wooden footbridge while keeping a sharp eye open for the grey wagtail and dipper which frequent the river hereabouts.

Cross two smaller bridges before emerging onto the minor road linking the B6049 in Miller's Dale with Litton Mill, about midway between the parish church of St Anne and the Angler's Rest Inn. Turn left for the few remaining yards to the B6049 and bus stop. For those being collected by car continue along the main road for over a quarter of a mile and, just beyond the craft workshop, turn right into the road signed to Wormhill. A short climb of 200 yards will take you to the National Park's car park on the site of the disused railway station.

19. Station to Village

This walk serves to illustrate that in the age of steam not all villages were
well served by their local station.

Route: Hartington station – Tissington Trail – White House Farm – Heathcote –
Hartington Hall – Hartington village.

Start: Hartington station. Map reference 149613. Altitude 360 metres.

Finish: Centre of Hartington village. Map reference 128604. Altitude 235 metres.

Distance: 2½ miles.

Duration: 1½ hours.

Map: The Peak District: White Peak Area, number 24 in the Ordnance Survey
Outdoor Leisure series.

Public Transport: Hartington station is served by a limited bus service from Ashbourne and Buxton on college days only. There is a limited service from Ashbourne
on Thursdays and Saturdays. On summer Sundays and Bank Holidays there are
buses from Huddersfield, Glossop, Sheffield, Chesterfield, Bakewell and Glossop.

Hartington village has daily buses to Buxton. There are buses from Leek on Mondays,
Wednesdays and Saturdays. There is a service from Hanley on Saturdays. On
Sundays and Bank Holidays there are buses from Sheffield, Chesterfield, Derby,
Mansfield, Bakewell, Ashbourne and Alfreton. On summer Sundays there is a service
from Rochdale, Ashton-under-Lyne, Glossop and Huddersfield.

By Car: Hartington station car park and picnic site is signed from the B5054 Newhaven–Longnor road, about ¼ mile from its junction with the A515. Hartington village
is also on the B5054; there is parking by the village pond and also in the car park.

Refreshments: Hartington village has a wide choice of pubs, serving bar meals, and
cafés.

Along the Way

Tissington Trail

The Tissington Trail is one of several routes created specially for walkers and cyclists by the Peak District National Park. It uses the bed of the former Buxton to Ashbourne Railway, which continued through to Uttoxeter, before it was axed in 1954. Hartington was a busy station, serving several local villages and sending daily supplies of milk to London. Today little remains of it except for a few railway artefacts and the signal box which serves as a National Park Information Centre, open at weekends.

Hartington Hall

Hartington

The village of Hartington earned for itself a mention in Domesday Book when it was valued at 40 shillings. It started to develop when it was given to William de Ferrers, who persuaded King John to grant a charter for a weekly market and a three-day fair to be held on the feast of St Giles, patron saint of the parish. Its importance was maintained when it passed into the ownership of the Duchy of Lancaster in the thirteenth century.

Little is heard of Hartington until the Civil War of the seventeenth century. A battle between Roundheads and Cavaliers on Hartington Moor left 600 corpses on the field. Shortly before this, in 1611, Hartington Hall was built by the Robert Bateman, a native of the village who flourished and made a fortune as a merchant in London. Charles II knighted his son and one member of the family rose, like Dick Whittington before him, to become Lord Mayor of London. The hall, typical of the Jacobean style of architecture, has mullioned windows and extending wings. Bateman's descendants continued to occupy it for three centuries but since the early 1930s it has been a very popular youth hostel.

Other ancient buildings include the church, built in the thirteenth and fourteenth centuries, the Devonshire Arms and the Old Market Hall, with its classical facade constructed in 1836.

The village has long been famous for its cheese. The present factory started operating more than a century ago but, by 1900, had ceased operating and lay derelict. It was bought and the business restarted by J. M. Nuttall who was responsible for introducing the manufacture of Stilton cheese. The factory just qualified because it lies a few yards within the Derbyshire boundary. In more recent times it has been acquired by Dairy Crest but still produces Stilton, Buxton Blue and Dovedale cheeses, all of which may be purchased in the Cheese Shop by the pond or mere.

The Route

Exit the car park southwards along the Tissington Trail but, 100 yards after the signal box, fork right along a path signed to Heathcote. Initially this takes the form of a walled lane but, over the first stile, develops into a field path with a limestone wall on the left.

By now an extensive panoramic view of the Upper Dove Valley has opened up to reveal Chrome Hill, one of three coral reefs in the area. Because of its mineral content it has given its name to the English language.

Beyond a second stile continue to the right of a wall to a squeezer stile by a five-barred gate; this is followed by a stone step stile and another squeezer before the path reverts to a lane with extremely low walls. In spring and early summer the air is filled with the trilling melodies of the skylark and, at any time of year, raucous crows wheel overhead.

On gaining a T-junction by White House Farm turn left and, keeping the farm on your right, advance a further 100 yards to the road through Heathcote hamlet. Cross into another narrow road displaying a cul-de-sac sign. After 100 yards turn right by a footpath post through the yard of Chapel Farm, staying just to the right of a wall and keeping the house on your left.

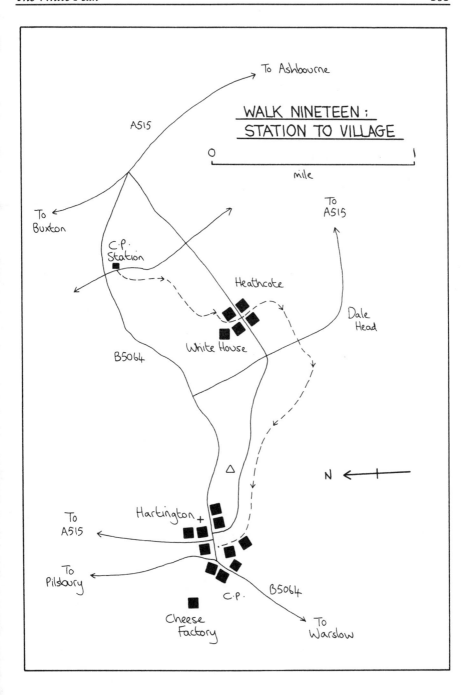

Where the yard ends with no apparent boundary of any kind maintain your line of direction across a field to a stone step stile adjacent to a five-barred gate. Stay to the right of the wall down the next field to an obvious stone step stile in the facing wall and so meet the minor road linking Hartington Dale with Dale End.

Cross the road into a facing walled lane, climbing a short distance to a T-junction. Turn right along another walled lane but, 250 yards after passing a splendid stone barn on your immediate left, and by a finger post, climb a stile on your left. Taking your direction from the arm of the footpath finger post, and staying close to the wall on your right, head towards a five-barred gate. Cross the next field by aiming for an obvious green gate in the facing wall and then stay forward to a second stile by a green gate, also recognisable by a footpath finger post.

With Hartington Hall youth hostel facing you, turn left. Proceed down the steep hill with the cheese factory's chimney prominent in the valley ahead and the parish church of St Giles to your right. On reaching the B5054 turn left into the village centre.

20. Motte and Bailey

A mainly riverside route which passes an ancient castle and reveals the glories of the Upper Dove.

Route: Crowdecote – Pilsbury Castle – Pilsbury – Hartington.

Start: The Packhorse Inn, Crowdecote. Map reference 101652. Altitude 253 metres.

Finish: Centre of Hartington village. Map reference 128604. Altitude 235 metres.

Distance: 4 miles.

Duration: 2 hours.

Map: The Peak District: White Peak Area, number 24 in the Ordnance Survey Outdoor Leisure series.

Public Transport: Crowdecote has buses from Leek and Bakewell on Mondays only.

Hartington has daily buses to Buxton. There are buses from Leek on Mondays, Wednesdays and Saturdays. There is a service from Hanley on Saturdays. On Sundays and Bank Holidays there are buses from Sheffield, Chesterfield, Derby, Mansfield, Bakewell, Ashbourne and Alfreton. On summer Sundays there is a service from Rochdale, Ashton-under-Lyne, Glossop and Huddersfield.

By Car: Crowdecote is on the road linking Longnor with the A515 at map reference 132659. In the absence of a car park parking can be difficult. Please ensure that you cause no obstructions.

Hartington is on the B5054 Newhaven–Longnor road and is signed from the A515. There is parking by the mere and also a car park.

Refreshments: The Packhorse Inn, Crowdecote, serves bar meals. There is a wide selection of pubs, serving bar food, and cafés in Hartington.

Along the Way

Crowdecote

This unusual name is derived from the Anglo-Saxon 'Cruda's Cot', 'Cruda' probably being a Saxon landowner and 'Cot' his hut or shelter. For centuries the hamlet was one of the recognised places for crossing the River Dove upstream of Hartington. The name of the adjacent pub, the Packhorse, originally a cottage in front of the present inn, is a reminder that it lay on the route from Bakewell and Monyash to Longnor and beyond.

The first bridge here was a simple wooden footbridge, replaced in 1709 by a stone packhorse one. When the road was turnpiked for the transport of chert from Hassop to Newcastle for use in the pottery industry, there was a toll bar station at Crowdecote.

Pilsbury Castle

This dates from the reign of William the Conqueror and was intended to keep the local tribes in order. It was a wooden structure of the motte and bailey type and appears never to have been rebuilt in stone.

Hartington

See Walk 19.

The Cheese Shoppe, Hartington

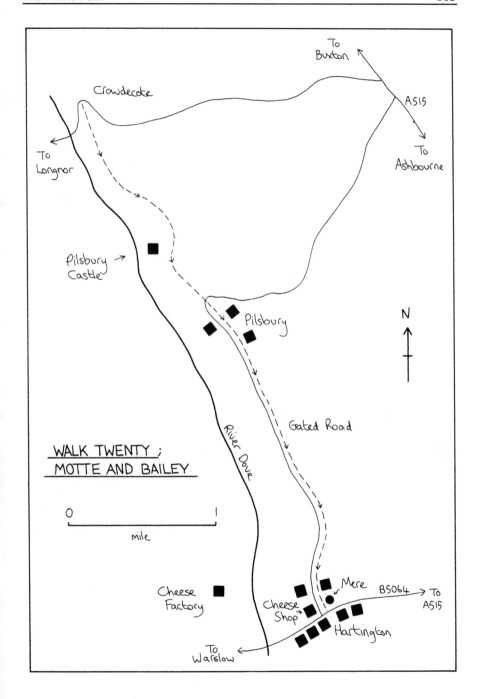

To
Buxton

A515

To
Ashbourne

Crowdecote

To
Longnor

Pilsbury
Castle

Pilsbury

N

Gated Road

River Dove

WALK TWENTY ;
MOTTE AND BAILEY

0   1

mile

Cheese
Factory

Cheese
Shop

Mere

B5064 → To
A515

Hartington

To
Warslow

The Route

Leave Crowdecote village by taking the dead-end road to the right of Toll Bar Cottage and, subsequently, a small terrace of stone cottages with an ornamental swan in the garden. Some 20 yards beyond, by the entrance to Bridge End Farm, fork right onto a track signed to Pilsbury and Sheen, so passing to the right of the farm.

At the next junction, after a mere 50 yards, stay forward through a squeezer stile as directed by a sign to Pilsbury. The path runs between a wall on your left and the River Dove a few yards away to your right. In sharp contrast to the reaches south of Hartington, the river here is a brown colour – a reminder that it has its source on the peat moorlands around Axe Edge.

Over a stone step stile the track runs between a wall on the left and a fence on the right but reverts to a field path after the next stile. It is idyllic in spring with curlew calling, skylark singing and the River Dove graced by mallard and moorhen as it negotiates a series of oxbow bends.

After passing through a gateway the path crosses directly over a stony track to a squeezer stile. Continue ahead through a long narrow field and over another stile to a footpath sign. Still continue forward, now on a track which ascends gently around the base of Pilsbury Castle to a stone step stile in the wall on your left. Turn right along the track for a quarter of a mile to reach a U-bend on a minor road in the tiny hamlet of Pilsbury.

Turn right along the narrow road signed to Hartington with a large imposing farmhouse set back on your left. Continue along this road, which is little better than surfaced lane as it passes through a succession of four five-barred gates to reach the pond in the centre of Hartington village. These gates deter many car drivers so the route is quiet as it undulates gently to pass Ludwell Farm, Bank Top Farm and Moot Hall Farm.

21. From Waterloo

This route, which uses field and riverside paths, is one of the most attractive in the Peak District.

Route: Biggin – Biggin Dale – Dovedale – Lode Mill – Milldale.

Start: The Waterloo Inn, Biggin. Map reference 804594. Altitude 336 metres.

Finish: Viator's Bridge, Milldale. Map reference 139547. Altitude 175 metres.

Distance: 4½ miles.

Duration: 2½ hours.

Map: The Peak District: White Peak Area, number 24 in the Ordnance Survey Outdoor Leisure series.

Public Transport: Biggin has buses from Hartington and Ashbourne on Thursdays and Saturdays and from Buxton on Saturdays, summer Sundays and Bank Holidays.

Milldale has a bus from Leek on Wednesdays.

By Car: Biggin and Milldale are both signed from the A515 Buxton–Ashbourne road south of Newhaven. There is roadside parking in Biggin. Milldale has a National Park car park.

Refreshments: The Waterloo Inn at Biggin serves bar meals. There is a café and shop in Milldale.

Along the Way

Biggin

The name of this remote village some two miles from Hartington means 'New Building'. It is best known for its sheep sales during the Autumn. These are the largest in the southern half of the White Peak, thousands of animals being sold every year.

The parish church of St Thomas is nineteenth-century while Biggin Hall, a small scale affair, dates from the seventeenth century.

Milldale

Milldale is one of the most popular spots in the Peak District, visitors being drawn there by the beauty of the valley but even more so by the old packhorse bridge and the associations with Charles Cotton and Izaak Walton (1593–1683). Viator's Bridge takes its name from one of the speakers in Walton's *Compleat Angler*.

Milldale itself, no more than a hamlet with mainly seventeenth- and eighteenth-century cottages, sits astride a packhorse route from Ashbourne to Alstonefield. Lode Mill, passed *en route*, is about half a mile further upstream.

Dale End

The Route

From the Waterloo Inn walk along the road in a westerly direction to the T-junction at Dale Head. Cross to a five-barred gate and negotiate the through stile alongside to enter Biggin Dale National Nature Reserve, which is cared for by English Nature.

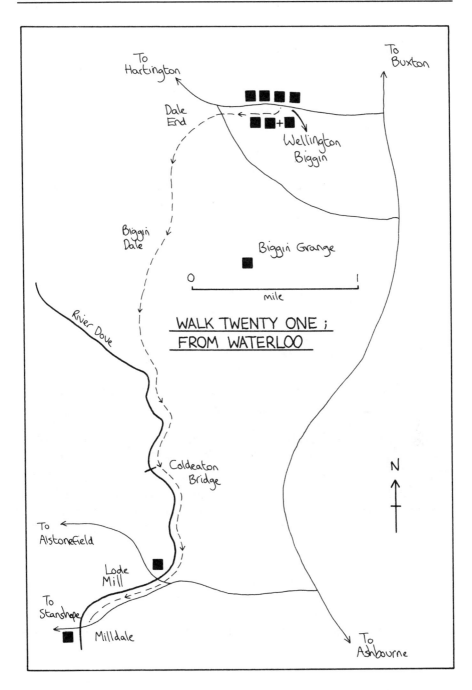

To Hartington

To Buxton

Dale End

Wellington Biggin

Biggin Dale

Biggin Grange

0   1
mile

River Dove

WALK TWENTY ONE ;
FROM WATERLOO

Coldeaton Bridge

N

To Alstonefield

Lode Mill

To Stanshope

Milldale

To Ashbourne

In its upper reaches the track is walled while the dale is blessed with gently sloping sides; the only blot on the landscape is a small sewage plant on your right after 250 yards. Beyond this the wall on the left disappears and the valley bends round to the left as the remaining wall terminates. The left-hand slope is well wooded with a mix of deciduous trees – from which the rooks maintain their incessant calls – while the clear path loses height gradually as it penetrates deeper into Biggin Dale with its rewarding views.

Negotiate a stone step stile and go forward a few yards to a footpath finger post, where a path from Hartington comes in from the right. Maintain your line of direction until nearing a facing wall backed by a very steep slope, which gives the appearance of blocking all further progress unless it is climbed. Have no fear: follow the path carefully as it surprisingly swings round to the left through a derelict wall to a small wooden gate, at the point where Biggin Dale forms a junction with another coming in from Dale Head on your left.

Through the gate turn sharp right to a finger post. By this make another right turn onto the bridleway signed Biggin Dale. Keep a concrete-lined pond on your right while carrying out these manoeuvres. There is now a wall on your immediate right as you head down Biggin Dale in a southerly direction; the wall soon turns south-eastwards for a short distance before reverting to a southerly line.

The dale is lined with harebells and red campion while the flanks are decked out in yellow gorse. After passing through a five-barred gate the wall is on your left and the flanks acquire a covering of hawthorn, hazel, and rowan from which emanate the calls of the green woodpecker, jay, magpie and a whole selection of woodland birds including blackbird, song thrush and robin.

Beyond a gateway the path becomes intermittently stony and rocky while passing occasional scree slopes and limestone outcrops. Eventually the bridleway forms a T-junction with the main riverside path through Dovedale opposite Peaseland Rocks at the southern end of Wolfscote Dale.

Turn left through the squeezer stile so that you are walking downstream with the River Dove on your right. In this stretch the river supports a population of mallard, dipper, moorhen, coot and grey wagtail. On quieter days – of which there are more than you may imagine – it may even be possible to catch glimpses of the somewhat elusive water vole swimming close to the far bank.

Clearly in view shortly after setting out downstream is Iron Tors, a cave on the left-hand slope. The Dove flows over a series of weirs specially constructed to facilitate the fishing for which it has been renowned since the days of Izaak Walton.

After more than half a mile a path joins from the left by Coldeaton Bridge. Eschew this, and the bridge, doggedly pursuing your course beyond a small stone building on your left, owned by Severn-Trent Water, and through a squeezer stile, as the river embarks on a rather large loop to the right and the woodlands on the left flank come to an end.

Proceed through further stiles until reaching one of the squeezer variety to the right of a white gate with a National Trust notice alongside. Pass an imposing stone house on your left before ascending a flight of eight stone steps to the side of a stone bridge, to reach the road from the A515 to Alstonefield at Lode Mill.

Turn right along the road to cross the bridge. Lode Mill, on the Staffordshire river bank, has had a somewhat chequered history, starting life as a lead smelting establishment before being transformed into a corn mill.

At the road junction fork left for the final half mile to the hamlet of Milldale and Viator's Bridge. This section of road walking is unavoidable: there is no riverside path, despite a campaign by the Ramblers' Association to persuade the National Trust to provide one. By Viator's Bridge follow the road round to the right to reach the National Park car park after some 200 yards.

22. Charles Cotton Country

Starting from one of the most picturesque villages in the Peak, we sample
the delights of another dry dale to reach Beresford Hall, former home of
Charles Cotton.

Route: Alstonefield – Narrowdale – Gratton Hill – Beresford Dale.

Start: National Park car park, Alstonefield. Map reference 131556. Altitude 277
metres.

Finish: Beresford Dale. Map reference 128586. Altitude 200 metres.

Distance: 2½ miles.

Duration: 1½ hours.

Map: The Peak District: White Peak Area, number 24 in the Ordnance Survey
Outdoor Leisure series.

Public Transport: Alstonefield has buses from Hartington and Ashbourne on Thursdays and Saturdays. There is a bus from Milldale and Leek on Wednesdays and one
from Macclesfield on occasional summer Sundays. There is also a bus from Mansfield, Derby and Ashbourne on summer Sundays and Bank Holidays.

There is no public transport to Beresford Dale.

By Car: Alstonefield is signed from the A515 south of Newhaven. It may also be
approached from the B5054 at Hulme End. There is a National Park car park.

Beresford Dale is signed from the B5054 between Hartington and Hulme End and
also from the Alstonefield–Hartington road. There is very restricted off-road parking.

Refreshments: The George in Alstonefield serves bar meals. There is also the Old
Post Office café in the village. Beresford Dale has no refreshments.

Along the Way

Alstonefield

Alstonefield has a history stretching back to early Christian times, perhaps
even further, for in 892 St Oswald, the Archbishop of York, dedicated a

church in the village. The large parish of 5,000 souls embraced Warslow and other villages including distant Quarnford, which must have meant that many parishioners rarely attended services.

After the Conquest Alstonefield became part of the property of Combermere Abbey in Cheshire, the monks exploiting it for wool and other produce. The present church, St Peter's, dates from the fifteenth century and is believed to be the third to occupy the site: it has a Norman doorway and arch which have survived all rebuilding, while inside, the Saxon stone crosses and font are thought to be survivals from the original church. There is also much splendid woodwork including a set of seventeenth-century pews, a double-decker pulpit and a gigantic wooden chest, once used for the storing of vestments and church silver.

Beresford Dale

Not only was Alstonefield an important ecclesiastical centre, it also benefited from being located at the junction of several ancient trackways. It enjoyed a weekly market as early as 1298 which was confirmed by a charter 10 years later. By Tudor times, however, the importance of the village had waned, the result of fierce competition from neighbouring Longnor, Hartington and Ashbourne. Nevertheless, it remained an important staging point on the packhorse network and coaching routes as testified by the building of the George Inn during the eighteenth century. The vicarage belongs to the same century but Alstonefield Hall predates both by 200 years.

During the late nineteenth century local farmers established a co-operative: their milk and cheese were produced in a building which still stands in Hopedale. Eventually, however, this venture went the same way as the village market. There used to be a wool market behind the George and a button factory. In more recent times, railways and main roads have steered clear of Alstonefield.

Beresford Hall

Beresford Hall, demolished in 1858, stood close by the finish of our walk. It was the home of Charles Cotton, friend of Izaak Walton, author of the *Compleat Angler*. The fishing house or temple constructed by Cotton still stands near the entrance to Beresford Dale but it is not accessible to the general public.

The Route

Turn left out of the National Park car park at Alstonefield. By the junction continue along the road signed to Hartington, passing the 'Old Reading Room', now a house, on your right and traffic de-restriction signs.

By the first bend to the left beyond the houses turn right up a short flight of three steps to a wooden stile, which is not identified by a footpath sign of any description. Walk diagonally to the left, aiming for a small wood with a derelict building; Low Plantation provides a summit on your right with a crown of trees.

The path carries you to a five-barred metal gate with a squeezer stile alongside in the wall on your left. Beyond the stile, resume the line of direction towards the corner of a wood; the rounded shape of Gratton Hill is obvious in the distance. Pass through another squeezer stile and continue along the same line, crossing a field corner to an obvious footpath finger post. Negotiate the adjacent squeezer stile before turning right along the walled lane: the imposing bulk of Narrowdale Hill lies away to your left, and the verges are lined with harebells. The surrounding plateau has several stone field barns creating a scene rather reminiscent of the Yorkshire Dales.

After 100 yards pass through a five-barred metal gate and, ignoring a waymarker just over the wall on your right, swing leftwards with the lane.

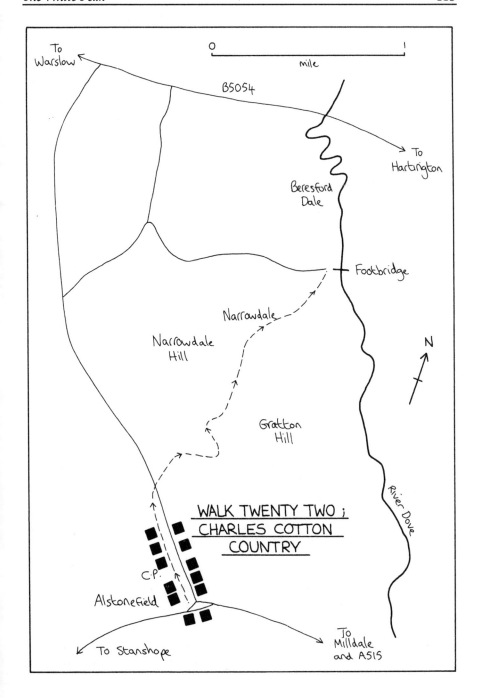

To Warslow

B5054

To Hartington

Beresford Dale

Footbridge

Narrowdale

Narrowdale Hill

N

Gratton Hill

River Dove

WALK TWENTY TWO ;
CHARLES COTTON
COUNTRY

C.P.

Alstonefield

To Stanshope

To Milldale and A515

mile

Twenty yards later it swings to the right, so providing an excellent view down Narrowdale.

Descend gradually to another five-barred gate with a wooden stile adjacent, which marks the end of the lane. Advance a few yards to an apparent junction and fork left along a broad grassy path which loses height rapidly with a wall on your right.

Where the wall corners to the right, swing right with it but, where it corners right a second time after 60 yards, continue forward towards the wall end in front. Narrowdale at this point is a wide, open valley, flanked on the left by the whale-like shape of Narrowdale Hill. On gaining the wall end, stay to the right of the wall to gain another metal five-barred gate with its accompanying wooden stile.

Still descending the dale, but with an easier gradient, pass to the right of a stone barn before negotiating a small metal gate. Beyond this all walls have disappeared and Narrowdale lives up to its name. Soon there are the remains of a small Lister pump engine set in a concrete base, complete with its wheel. One is left wondering why it was ever erected in this lonely spot.

Beyond the next squeezer stile you meet an intersection of tracks. Ignore the first on the right which heads up the slope and is not marked on the map as a right of way. Rather maintain your general line of direction by going ahead to walk with a wall on your left. Narrowdale Farm is a short distance up the track to the left.

After 100 yards a five-barred gate provides entry to a walled lane which transforms into a mere track after a short distance. Continue along this with a wall on your left to negotiate more gates. This landscape has markedly more trees than earlier in the walk, with hedgerows showing a tendency to supplant drystone walls.

After a succession of stone step stiles the wall on your left is replaced by a fence, before you cross a culverted stream to enter the northern reaches of Wolfscote Dale. The track soon becomes lined with hawthorn as it drops towards a stone step stile. Cross that, and turn right to the footbridge spanning the River Dove. This is the northern stretch of the Dove between Thorpe and Hartington, and the point where Wolfscote Dale meets Beresford Dale.

At this point you can be met by car or, if you wish, continue through Beresford Dale along the well-trodden and signed footpath to Hartington.

23. By Hall Dale

One of the finest approaches to Dovedale, this walk uses a mixture of field paths and tracks.

Route: Alstonefield – Dale Bottom – Stanshope – Grove Farm – Hall Dale – Ilam Rock – Milldale.

Start: National Park car park, Alstonefield. Map reference 131556. Altitude 277 metres.

Finish: Viator's Bridge, Milldale. Map reference 139547. Altitude 175 metres.

Distance: 3¾ miles.

Duration: 2 hours.

Map: The Peak District: White Peak Area, number 24 in the Ordnance Survey Outdoor Leisure series.

Public Transport: Alstonefield has buses from Hartington and Ashbourne on Thursdays and Saturdays. There is a bus from Milldale and Leek on Wednesday and one from Macclesfield on occasional summer Sundays. There is also a bus from Mansfield, Derby and Ashbourne on summer Sundays and Bank Holidays.

Milldale has a bus from Leek on Wednesdays.

By Car: Alstonefield is signed from the A515 south of Newhaven. It may also be approached from the B5054 at Hulme End. There is a National Park car park.

Milldale is signed from the A515 south of Newhaven. It may also be approached by a minor road from Alstonefield. There is a National Park car park.

Refreshments: The George in Alstonefield serves bar meals. There is the Old Post Office café in Alstonefield and another in Milldale.

Along the Way

Alstonefield

See Walk 22.

Milldale

See Walk 21.

Stanshope

Stanshope Hall was built during Tudor times by John Jackson, in whose family it remained until 1767 when it was bought by a Chesterfield money lender named Manley. When he was declared bankrupt, the Hall was left empty and fell into a state of dereliction until rescued and restored during the nineteenth century.

Viator's Bridge, Milldale

The Route

From the car park entrance turn right along the road. At the first junction go right again to another junction within yards. Cross the road to walk to the left of the small village green to meet another road. Turn left but, almost at once, turn left into a lane between cottages, one having a fancy gate incorporating a wheel.

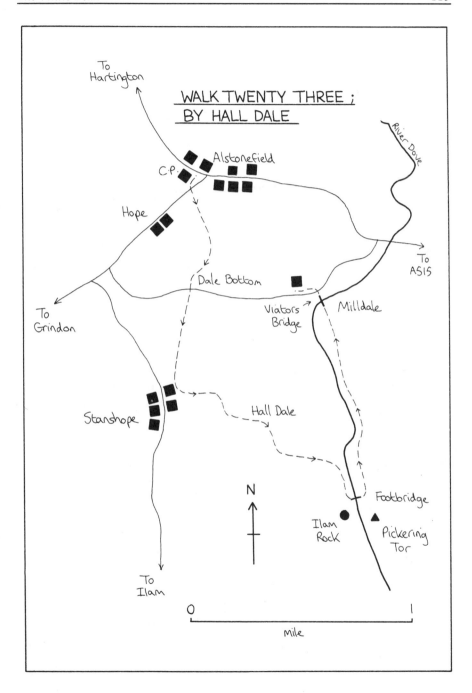

To
Hartington

WALK TWENTY THREE ;
BY HALL DALE

River Dove

Alstonefield

C.P.

Hope

To
A515

Dale Bottom

To
Grindon

Viators
Bridge

Milldale

Stanhope

Hall Dale

N

Footbridge

Ilam
Rock

Pickering
Tor

To
Ilam

0   1

Mile

A few yards after entering the lane a footpath finger post is encountered on your left and a stone barn is reached, also on your left. The lane bends to the right 10 yards afterwards.

At this point stay forward through a squeezer stile by a five-barred gate, continuing in the same direction over the field with a wall on your right to negotiate a gap between the walls in the field corner. Through this bear right, while still remaining to the left of a wall in a small, narrowing field, to reach a stile in the apex.

Stay to the left of the wall in descending a steep-sided dale adorned with ragwort and thistles. Where this wall corners to the right follow the path as it drops to a squeezer stile at Dale Bottom on the road linking Milldale with Hopedale.

Cross this minor road into the lane almost directly opposite for a steepish climb through harebells and red campion for approximately a quarter mile. Having passed a stone barn on your left the gradient eases considerably before levelling by Grove Farm to emerge by a tiny green onto the minor road through the hamlet of Stanshope.

Turn left and immediately left again into another lane, this time signed to Milldale. After 100 yards turn right through a squeezer stile with a sign reading 'Dovedale one mile'. Cross the corner of the field to a stone step stile in the wall on your left and then turn diagonally right, gradually moving further away from the wall.

Beyond another stile, decorated with a waymarker, go forward to a stone step stile before heading down Hall Dale, a most attractive green valley. After 35 yards negotiate another stone step stile by a National Trust notice. The flanks are peppered with small limestone outcrops and the turf path is gentle on the feet as you descend gradually through a green landscape.

Beyond the next stile the right flank acquires a covering of pines which, in turn, gives way to mixed broad-leaved trees. Overhead there is the call of rooks. Soon the dale narrows and the downward gradient steepens until you traverse a patch of level turf onto the Staffordshire bank of the River Dove.

Turn right through a stile to follow the riverside path downstream for a quarter mile to Ilam Rock, a towering limestone buttress much favoured by climbers. Turn left over the footbridge to the base of Pickering Tor and left again to follow the Dove upstream on the Derbyshire bank. Along this stretch you will pass Doveholes, a set of caves, and Ravens' Tor, although no such birds are now in evidence.

After passing through three small gates *en route* you will finally arrive at Viator's Bridge. Turn left and, at the far end, you will be in the hamlet of Milldale where a visit to the National Trust Information Shelter will prove most enlightening.

24. To the Southern Tip

This makes for a pleasant amble, completely on field paths, close to the southern border of the National Park.

Route: Tissington – Bassett Wood Farm – Fenny Bentley.

Start: National Park car park on the Tissington Trail, Tissington. Map reference 178521. Altitude 229 metres.

Finish: The Coach and Horses Inn, Fenny Bentley. Map reference 175501. Altitude 136 metres.

Distance: 1¾ miles.

Duration: 1 hour.

Map: The Peak District: White Peak Area, number 24 in the Ordnance Survey Outdoor Leisure series.

Public Transport: Tissington village has buses from Ashbourne and Ilam on Thursdays and Saturdays. There are buses to Tissington Gates on the A515, approximately half a mile from the start, from Buxton, Mansfield, Ashbourne and Derby on summer Sundays and Bank Holidays.

Fenny Bentley has buses from Ashbourne, Hartington and Ilam on Thursdays and Saturdays.

By Car: Tissington village is signed from the A515 between Ashbourne and Newhaven. Car park by Tissington Trail.

Fenny Bentley is on the A515 two miles north of Ashbourne. Parking off-road but limited.

Refreshments: The Old School House in Tissington village serves light meals and snacks daily from Easter to the end of October. The Coach and Horses Inn, Fenny Bentley, serves bar meals.

Along the Way

Tissington

Many people regard Tissington as the most picturesque village in the

National Park, a claim that is hard to dispute. It is dominated by the Hall, with its long facade standing back from and slightly above the road. The core dates from the early seventeenth century with extensive additions in 1896.

The manor of Tissington was given by William the Conqueror to William de Ferrers and it was transferred subsequently into the ownership of other families until, in 1460, it passed to the Fitzherberts who still live there.

The parish church, standing on slightly raised ground facing the Hall, is of Norman origin with later additions. The Norman archway, chancel and font still survive, rubbing shoulders with an Elizabethan pulpit, box pews, a two-decker pulpit from the eighteenth century and memorials to various members of the Fitzherbert family. The Old Church House has survived from the late seventeenth century but most of the cottages were constructed during the mid-nineteenth century.

Thanks to the policies of the Fitzherberts, the village has escaped some of the scourges of the twentieth century such as leisure complexes and commuter housing developments. This is a closely knit community, where young people are not compelled to leave in search of housing elsewhere.

Tissington is renowned for its annual well-dressing ceremony which takes place on Ascension Thursday . Five wells are decorated with flowers as a reminder that the village has never suffered from a shortage of water. It is believed that Tissington introduced the well-dressing custom to the Peak District: it may have its origin in pagan customs, or the great drought of 1615, when little or no rain fell between 25 March and 4 August.

Fenny Bentley

The most notable feature of Fenny Bentley is the Old Hall, now known as Cherry Orchard Farm. Parts of it are medieval and parts Jacobean. It is unique in the Peak District by virtue of having a pele tower, after the fashion of similar fortified houses along the English and Scottish borders. Its most exceptional occupant was Sir Thomas Beresford who fathered 21 children, all of whom pre-deceased him. He sent a complete troop of horse, including his 16 sons and many of his retainers, to fight at Agincourt.

The parish church, dedicated to St Edmund, King and Martyr, has an unusual carving to the left of the door into the chancel. It shows a fox carrying off a goose. This is believed to refer to the Dean of Lincoln who took more than his fair share of the money collected in tithes by the parish of Fenny Bentley. Very little remains of the Norman church which can be authenticated. The main parts of the building are in the Perpendicular style of the fourteenth century with later additions and alterations, especially in the nineteenth century. The most notable feature is the Beresford Chapel containing the figures of Sir Thomas Beresford, his wife and their 21 children, almost totally enclosed with shrouds. There is also a fine late fifteenth-century wooden screen.

Fenny Bentley Hall

The Route

Leave by the car park exit before turning right along the road to Bradbourne. Go through a pair of gateposts, over the stone bridge spanning the Tissington Trail, and over a cattle grid. Immediately turn right by an armless footpath post to cross a small patch of rough grass to a five-barred gate. In the absence of a stile proceed through this and maintain your line of direction to the diagonally opposite field corner.

You will see that in this southern extremity of the White Peak hedges appear to have replaced drystone walls. As you approach the field corner you will observe a circular salmon-pink marker disc ahead. On reaching it turn left

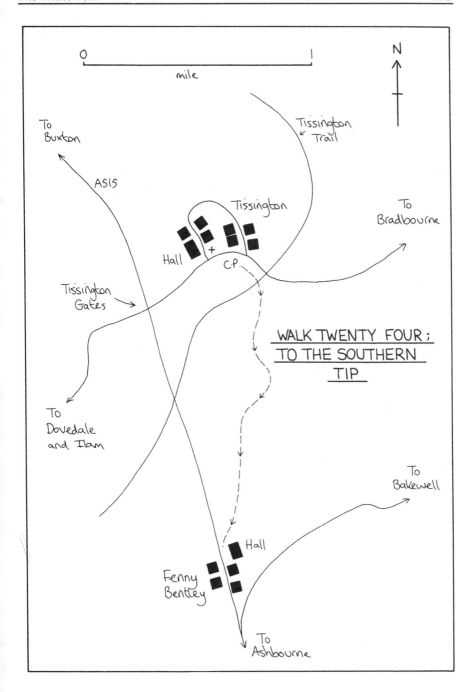

WALK TWENTY FOUR;
TO THE SOUTHERN
TIP

through a squeezer stile and stay to the left of a hedge, while crossing another large field to a wooden stile with another pink disc.

Exit onto the approach drive to Bassett Wood Farm. Turn right to pass through two metal gates and beneath overhead wires. A short distance before reaching the farmhouse, turn left over a stile with a yellow way-marker. The small grass lump to your left is a prehistoric tumulus. Cross the centre of the field to a wooden stile, picked out by another yellow disc, some 15 yards to the right of a five-barred gate. At this point you catch a tantalising glimpse of Thorpe Cloud, the 'Guardian of Dovedale', away to your right.

In crossing the next field, also very large, take a bearing on another yellow disc in the far right-hand corner. Pass through a gate before continuing the final descent of the Pennines towards the Midlands Plain, while staying to the left of a hedge which is host to thistles, nettles and dandelions.

Guided by yet another yellow disc continue down the rather long field to a wooden stile in the bottom left-hand corner by a holly tree. Stay forward, passing a small wooden partial enclosure to your left while homing in on a hedge corner. Beyond this continue to the next hedge corner, which has a pylon alongside sending wires in three directions. Turn right by this to pass a pebbledashed house on your right and, after 12 yards, join a broad track. Negotiate a small wooden gate and continue down the lane, which is now flanked by houses.

Cross a small stone bridge to a T-junction by the old school, which is now a base for Boy Scouts. Turn left to pass to the right of Fenny Bentley Old Hall before meeting the A515. Turn left for the few remaining yards to the Coach and Horses.

25. Turnpike and Trail

Another walk through the southern extremity of the Pennines, following a modern trail and an ancient turnpike.

Route: Tissington – Thorpe – Coldwall Bridge – Ilam.

Start: National Park car park by the Tissington Trail, Tissington. Map reference 178521. Altitude 229 metres.

Finish: National Trust car park, Ilam Hall. Map reference 132506. Altitude 147 metres.

Distance: 4½ miles.

Duration: 2½ hours.

Maps: 1. The Peak District: White Peak Area, number 24 in the Ordnance Survey Outdoor Leisure series.
2. Buxton, Matlock and Dovedale, Sheet number 119 in the Ordnance Survey Landranger series.
3. Ashbourne and the Churnet Valley, Sheet SK 04/14, number 810 in the Ordnance Survey Pathfinder series.

Public Transport: Tissington village has buses from Ashbourne and Ilam on Thursdays and Saturdays. Tissington Gates on the A515 (½ mile from the start) has buses from Buxton, Mansfield, Ashbourne and Derby on summer Sundays and Bank Holidays.

Ilam has a bus from Leek on Wednesdays and from Ashbourne on Thursdays and Saturdays. On summer Sundays and Bank Holidays there are buses from Mansfield, Derby, Alfreton and Ashbourne.

By Car: Tissington village is signed from the A515 between Ashbourne and Newhaven. National Park car park. Ilam is reached by minor roads from the A515 at Tissington Gates and also from the A523 at Calton Moor. It is signed in both cases. Car park at Ilam Hall.

Refreshments: The Old School House Tea Room, Tissington, serves light meals and snacks daily between Easter and the end of October. The Manifold café in the country park at Ilam also serves meals and light refreshments. There are pubs in Thorpe serving bar meals.

Along the Way

Tissington

See Walk 24.

Ilam

During the Middle Ages the land now surrounding Ilam was owned by the Benedictine abbey of Burton-upon-Trent, but Ilam's ecclesiastical history goes back many centuries earlier. St Bertram, allegedly the son of a king of the Midland kingdom of Mercia, travelled to Ireland where he married a princess. On their way home with their baby daughter they were sheltering in a forest when Bertram went to seek help. On his return he found both mother and daughter had been killed by wolves. Consequently he lived the life of a hermit near Ilam and converted many pagans to Christianity.

He is buried in Ilam church where, for centuries, his shrine has attracted pilgrims, some of whom still leave their written requests. The packhorse bridge over the Manifold in the grounds of Ilam Hall is named after him, and his well is to be found on Bunster Hill.

Ilam Church

The earliest church was erected in Saxon times, from which period dates the stone cross in the churchyard. The present building was erected in 1618 and substantially altered in the nineteenth century.

The focal point of Ilam, however, is the Hall, where the Restoration playwright Congreve (1670–1729) spent many of his early years and where he wrote *The Old Bachelor*, his first successful play. His 'study', a grotto in the grounds complete with stone table and chair, may still be seen. Dr Johnson was also a visitor. Jesse Watts-Russell extensively remodelled the Hall in imitation of Alton Towers during the early Victorian period, when he also erected many of the Swiss-type houses still to be seen in the village. In this century the Hall was given to the National Trust for specific use as a youth hostel.

The tall, slender and elaborately carved monument which stands at the road junction in the centre of Ilam was erected in honour of Mary, the wife of Watts-Russell, in 1840.

Coldwall Bridge

Stands on the Thorpe to Blythe turnpike road, authorised in 1762. A few yards on the Thorpe side of the bridge is an old milestone.

Thorpe

The name is of Scandinavian origin being translated as 'farmstead'. The church is of Norman origin with a low, square tower, but may occupy the site of an even earlier one. The font is unusual in that it takes the shape of a tub: it is one of three of this type in the county, all believed to date from the eleventh century. Examined carefully, the stonework on either side of the porch bears evidence that arrows were sharpened there during the medieval period, when all able-bodied men were expected to practise their archery every Sunday.

The Route

From the car park at Tissington head south along the Tissington Trail. The embankments and cuttings are carpeted with colourful patches of rosebay willowherb, red campion, meadow cranesbill, ox-eye daisies, birdsfoot trefoil, purple-headed thistles, viper's bugloss, common ragwort, white and purple clovers, dandelions and a whole variety of umbellifers.

Cross a small bridge over a path, then go underneath a metal bridge carrying

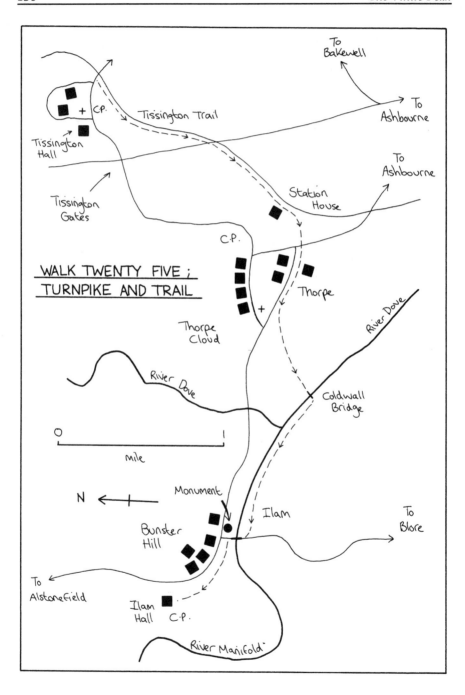

To
Bakewell

To
Ashbourne

Tissington Trail

C.P.

Tissington
Hall

To
Ashbourne

Tissington
Gates

Station
House

C.P.

WALK TWENTY FIVE ;
TURNPIKE AND TRAIL

Thorpe

River Dove

Thorpe
Cloud

River Dove

Coldwall
Bridge

O   I

mile

N

Monument

Ilam

To
Blore

Bunster
Hill

To
Alstonefield

Ilam
Hall   C.P.

River Manifold

the A515 followed by a well-proportioned arched bridge to reach Thorpe picnic area which is the first south of Tissington and has the Old Station House to your right.

Continue with the Trail for a further 100 yards before turning right through a wooden kissing gate onto a path signed to Dovedale. Take your direction from the yellow waymarker while keeping well to the left of a large tree as you climb gently for the short distance to the dome of the field. From there head for a stone squeezer stile some five yards to the right of a pylon.

Veer 10 degrees to the right, passing beneath overhead wires to a wooden stile which gives onto a narrow road by a T-junction. Cross directly into the facing road, passing through a gateway as you do so. After 20 yards a house called The Firs is on your left while the distinctive form of Thorpe Cloud is directly ahead.

Pay no attention to a footpath on your left signed to Mapleton and Ashbourne. Continue along the road, passing to the right of a farm to begin a steep descent. At the bottom of the dip, about seven yards beyond a telegraph pole, turn left by a footpath sign before dropping a few yards to cross a narrow stream. On the far bank turn left to a white notice, indicating dangerous marshes on either side of the wide path.

Climb gradually through the trees, staying to the right of a low, moss-covered wall. The ground flora include wood anemones, celandine, wild garlic and ground ivy. Having passed to the left of St Leonard's Church in Thorpe the path forms a T-junction with a lane on a bend. Go forward, and after a short distance along the lane a road lined with houses is reached.

Turn left but, after 20 yards and by Ivy Cottage, turn right into a grassy walled lane signed as a public footpath. After 100 yards negotiate a stone squeezer stile and, where the lane ends, maintain direction for approximately 75 yards over grass to a footpath sign standing in isolation by a broad track.

Turn right along what was once the Thorpe to Blythe Marsh Turnpike for a long gradual descent into the valley of the River Dove. As you do so you are rewarded by a wonderful extensive vista of rolling rounded hills dotted with cattle and sheep with scattered woodlands adding to the variety.

After approximately half a mile of descent there is a milestone on the left with a cast-iron panel inset which reads 'Cheadle 11', a relic of the turnpike days. Continue over the substantial Coldwall Bridge spanning the Dove, passing through a five-barred gate. After about 100 yards and by a footpath sign, turn right through a squeezer stile to follow the path signed to 'Ilam 1 mile'.

Pass through a few trees into the open field. In the absence of a clearly defined path on the ground aim for a small waymarker post, heading slightly to the right as you dip into a hollow, and pass through a metal five-barred gate before climbing to a distant but obvious footpath finger post.

Beyond this post maintain your direction over a very large field towards another finger post by a clump of hawthorns, from where there is a good view into the southern entrance of the Dovedale of the tourist. By this post turn right downhill along what has by now developed into a very distinct footpath as it pursues its course through more hawthorns.

After 100 yards, and by a waymark, veer right towards another waymarker post which is reached after 150 yards. Stay forward to a wooden stile by a holly tree and then maintain direction through the trees to yet another waymarker before descending to a wooden footbridge with a stile at the far end.

At this point the route joins the River Manifold close to its confluence with the Dove. Beyond the footbridge, stay forward along the riverside path to a stile and then pass beneath overhead wires before crossing a single plank footbridge.

Cross two further footbridges before circling round the field boundary to a flight of five steps, at the top of which you emerge onto the Blore end of Ilam bridge. Turn right over the bridge and, with a view of Bunster Hill directly ahead, keep to the left of the stone memorial. Where the road bends to the right stay forward for 20 yards before veering left by a sign to the church. After 20 yards, and by the entrance to Dovedale House, turn left through a metal kissing gate.

Walk to the left of the boundary wall of Dovedale House but, where this ends, go left for 50 yards and then right to pass the north side of the church to the National Trust car park at Ilam Hall.

26. Close to Thor

While not actually visiting Thor's Cave, this route offers excellent views of the geological phenomenon.

Route: Wetton – Manifold Trail – Weag's Bridge.

Start: Car park, Wetton village. Map reference 109552. Altitude 291 metres.

Finish: Weag's Bridge. Map reference 100541. Altitude 160 metres.

Distance: 2¼ miles.

Duration: 1¼ hours.

Map: The Peak District: White Peak Area, number 24 in the Ordnance Survey Outdoor Leisure series.

Public Transport: Wetton has buses from Ashbourne on Thursdays and Saturdays. There is no public transport to Weag's Bridge.

By Car: Wetton is approached by minor roads from Ilam, Alstonefield or Hulme End on the B5054. There is a National Park car park in the village. Weag's Bridge is approached by minor roads from Wetton or Grindon, and has a small car park.

Refreshments: Ye Olde Royal Oak Inn, Wetton, serves bar meals. There is also the Tea Rooms in Wetton.

Along the Way

Wetton

This attractive village on the limestone plateau has a history dating back to at least Roman times. Excavations near the village have revealed what experts believe to be the site of a Romano-British settlement, with foundations of houses along with pottery, a skeleton, a Roman coin and two bars of lead.

At Long Low, about a mile from the village, other excavations have revealed the presence of man in the Early Bronze Age. Discoveries there included 13 human skeletons along with the bones of oxen, pigs, dogs and deer.

The present village, probably occupying the site of an earlier one, contains splendid examples of vernacular architecture from the seventeenth and eighteenth centuries. The parish church of St Margaret is of simple design with a fourteenth-century tower.

Thor's Cave

Thor's Cave is a natural cavity high on the hillside above the Manifold Valley. Evidence of early human occupation has been found in the form of flint arrowheads, bone combs, bronze brooches and Roman pottery.

Manifold Valley Light Railway

This narrow gauge railway was built in 1904 with a view to carrying coal and milk to the creamery at Hulme End. Another incentive was the possibility of re-opening the copper mines at Ecton. As this never happened, the railway was an economic failure from the outset and was closed after 30 years. Eight miles in length, it ran through some of the most attractive scenery in the Peak District from Waterhouses in the south to Hulme End in the north. The locomotives of the railway were imitations of those used in India and were fitted with cow catchers. Some of the former railway buildings are still preserved at Waterhouses and Hulme End.

Most of the track has been converted into a walking trail although one section, between Wetton Mill and Swainsley, has been adapted as the county road, leaving the original to decline into a bridleway.

The Route

Leave the car park in Wetton by the end nearest the village and immediately turn left over a stone step stile with a finger post alongside plus another indicating the Tea Rooms ahead. With St Margaret's Church away to your right, follow a wide track across rough grazing ground some 200 yards to a metal stile.

Continue through the buildings of Carr Farm before turning left over a stone step stile by an asbestos building to walk a further 15 yards between close walls to a squeezer stile. This permits access to a road leading to Wetton Mill.

By Carr Farm entrance turn left along the road (or right if you wish to visit the Tea Rooms or the pub) to pass a large concrete pond (or open-air swimming pool?) on your left by New House Farm.

After 70 yards a T-junction on a bend is reached and easily recognised by a

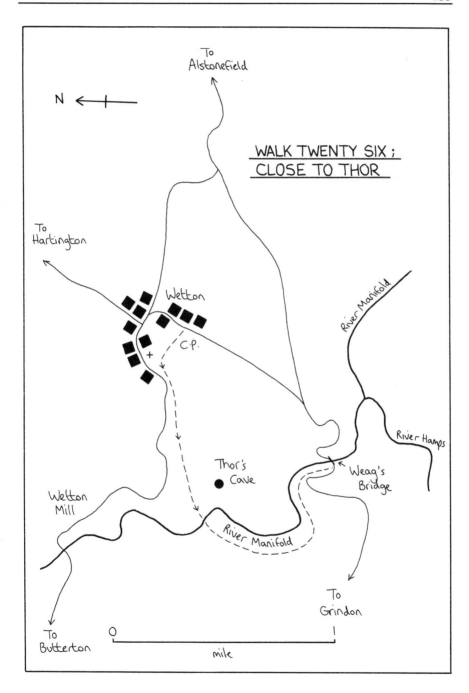

To
Alstonefield

N ←──┼──

WALK TWENTY SIX ;
CLOSE TO THOR

To
Hartington

Wetton

River Manifold

C.P.

River Hamps

Thor's
Cave

Weag's
Bridge

Wetton
Mill

River Manifold

To
Grindon

0   1

To
Butterton

mile

blue sign with white lettering which reads 'Single Track Road with Passing Places'. Turn right, eschew a lane on the left after 20 yards marked as a concessionary footpath, and continue a further 10 yards before making a left turn through a squeezer stile signed 'Thor's Cave, ½ mile'. After a somewhat muddy start, take a bearing on the spire of Grindon church which is conspicuous on the far side of the Manifold Valley. Descend gradually down the centre of a very long field towards a gateway beside a yellow waymarker pole. Beyond this maintain your line of direction down the centre of a valley with the loss of altitude accentuated. Given a good snow cover this would make an excellent ski slope.

Ignore any side paths which may tempt you. With a very good view of Thor's Cave above to your left, negotiate a wooden squeezer stile to enter woodland. The clear though muddy path continues downhill to another wooden squeezer stile followed, within 20 yards, by a concrete footbridge over the usually dry bed of the River Manifold.

At the far end fork left to reach the surfaced Manifold Trail. Turn left along this by a National Trust sign. Ossom's Hill is to your right. Proceed along the Trail through delightful woodlands, which afford cool shade on sunny days while providing a chorus of mixed birdsong and a display of wild flowers including butterbur with its gigantic leaves, red campion and meadow cranesbill. After almost a mile the car park at Weag's Bridge is reached, making this a perfect short downhill walk.

27. Down to the Mill

A very pleasant if somewhat muddy walk along field paths.

Route: Butterton – The Ford – Hoo Brook – Waterslacks – Wetton Mill.

Start: The road junction by the church, Butterton. Map reference 075566. Altitude 296 metres.

Finish: Wetton Mill. Map reference 097561. Altitude 165 metres.

Distance: 2 miles.

Duration: 1 hour.

Map: The Peak District: White Peak Area, number 24 in the Ordnance Survey Outdoor Leisure series.

Public Transport: Butterton has occasional buses from Leek, Buxton and Hartington. Ring Busline for details.

Wetton Mill is served by the Manifold Valley Light Railway minibus service from Hulme End on Sundays during July. At Hulme End there are connections with Hartington, Congleton, Newcastle, Hanley, Macclesfield, Mansfield and Derby. Details from the Peak Park Planning Board (0629 814321).

By Car: Butterton is signed from the B5053 which links Warslow to Bottom House on the A523 Leek to Ashbourne road. Limited off-road parking by the church.

Wetton Mill may be approached from Butterton, Grindon or Hulme End on the B5054. There is a National Park car park. Parking also for patrons of the café at Wetton Mill.

Refreshments: The Gallery Restaurant in Butterton. The Lion Inn, Butterton, serves bar meals. There is a café at Wetton Mill.

Along the Way

Butterton

The tall spire of Butterton church is a landmark for miles around. Dedicated to St Bartholomew, it is one of the newest in the Peak District, having been built as recently as the nineteenth century. However, inside it does have some earlier 'Commandment Boards' and a church register used since 1670. There is also a plaque to Joseph Wood, Rowland Cantrell and William Hambleton, who died in an unsuccessful attempt to rescue Joseph Shenton from an unused mine shaft in 1842.

The village itself has always been isolated and devoted mainly to a grazing economy. It straggles along the main street downhill to a ford over Hoo Brook.

The Ford, Butterton

Wetton Mill

Wetton Mill was set up by William Cavendish, a son of Bess of Hardwick, and remained in the ownership of the Devonshire family until the early seventeenth century. It ceased operations in 1857 and part of it has now been converted into a café. Behind the mill is the Minor Rock Shelter where artefacts from various prehistoric periods have been unearthed. The present stone buildings date from the eighteenth century.

The Route

Start from the road junction near the church with roads leading off to Ecton and Hulme End, Grindon and the B5053. Take the one which runs between the church of St Bartholomew, with its very tall steeple, and the Black Lion Inn which is on your right and carries a plaque over the entrance bearing the inscription:

M
W & G
1782

The road descends steeply to a T-junction. Turn left for an even more rapid descent while passing the Gallery Restaurant on your left. At the bottom of the hill cross the narrow stone bridge over Hoo Brook. Then turn left along the pavement so that both the brook and the ford are on your left. Walk alongside the ford for several yards but, part way along, turn left to cross the road, walking through the shallow water, to enter a lane marked by a waymark that is far from easy to spot.

After 50 yards, and facing a cottage, go to the right over a stream and take the narrow path for 20 yards to a wooden stile. Turn left through a gateway with Hoo Brook on your left. The stream will be your constant companion for some distance.

Stay close to the fence on your left while crossing the bottom of a sloping field. Negotiate an unusual type of wooden squeezer stile, pass beneath overhead power lines, keep a wall on your left and, immediately over the next stile, cross a small tributary stream flowing in from the right.

Advance for about 50 yards by the very edge of Hoo Brook to a clump of hawthorns. Turn left over a set of stepping stones to a wooden stile reached by a flight of three stone steps. By the adjacent wooden footpath finger post turn right so that Hoo Brook is now to your right.

After approximately 80 yards climb a wooden stile to keep forward, through a collapsed stone wall followed by a gap in a row of hawthorns, to reach the confluence of Hoo Brook with the stream flowing in from Grindon. Negotiate a facing wooden stile and turn left to cross a tiny wooden footbridge onto a wide grass path.

The well-wooded slopes of Ossoms Hill are to your right. Beyond another stile the valley bends to the right, while the path reaches a set of waymarks offering a choice between a footpath and a bridleway. Fork right along the

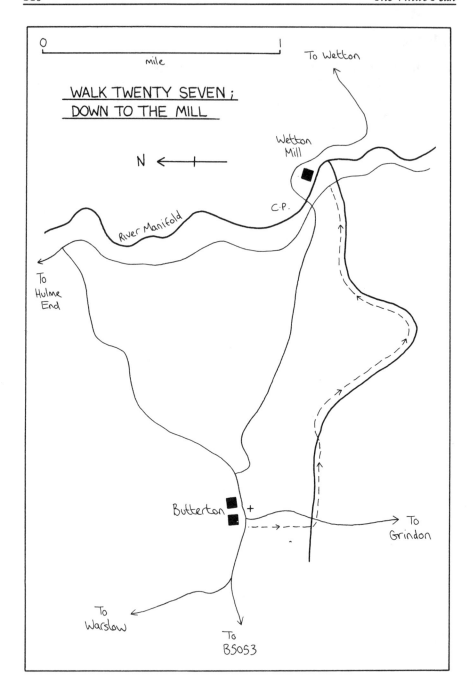

WALK TWENTY SEVEN ;
DOWN TO THE MILL

path but, after approximately 100 yards and facing the barrier of a five-barred gate, turn left up a short flight of wooden steps to another footpath post.

Turn right over a stile onto a wide track with a chatter surface with Wetton Hill looming directly ahead. Pass to the left of the campsite to a wooden five-barred gate which affords an exit onto the Wetton–Butterton road. Turn right for the 15 yards to its junction with the main valley road and cross the facing stone bridge over the Manifold to Wetton Mill and the café. If not wanting refreshments turn left at the road junction for the car park.

28. To the Southern Terminus

A pleasant route from the uplands of the White Peak plateau to the lowlands and southern terminus of the Manifold Valley Light Railway. Mainly on tracks and field paths.

Route: Grindon – Little Wood – Lee House – Manifold Trail – Waterhouses.

Start: National Park car park, Grindon. Map reference 085545. Altitude 316 metres.

Finish: National Park car park, Waterhouses. Map reference 085502. Altitude 220 metres.

Distance: 3½ miles.

Duration: 2 hours.

Map: The Peak District: White Peak Area, number 24 in the Ordnance Survey Outdoor Leisure series.

Public Transport: Grindon has buses from Leek and Waterhouses on Wednesdays and Saturdays.

Waterhouses has frequent daily buses from Manchester, Stockport, Macclesfield, Leek, Ashbourne and Derby.

By Car: Grindon may be approached by a minor road from the A523 at Waterhouses and minor roads from Wetton (see Walk 26) and Alstonefield (see Walk 22). National Park car park by the church. Waterhouses is on the A523 road about midway between Leek and Ashbourne; National Park car park on the site of the former railway station.

Refreshments: The Cavalier Inn at Grindon and several pubs in Waterhouses serve bar meals.

Along the Way

Grindon

Grindon is another rather isolated village on the limestone plateau of the southern White Peak and officially within the boundary of the Staffordshire Moorlands. As with neighbouring Butterton (see Walk 27) it lay on pack-horse routes carrying ore from the copper mines at Ecton – this probably explains why the former name of the present pub, the Cavalier, was the Smithy. It is the last remaining pub in the village, the other having vanished along with the post office, school and shop. The remains of the pinfold are opposite the Cavalier.

The Rindle Stone, Grindon

Known as the 'Cathedral of the Moorlands', Grindon parish church was completed in 1848. There are reminders of the church which occupied the site earlier in the form of two stone charnel coffins, the stone font and the medieval glass windows. Amongst the memorials is one to the crew of an RAF plane which crashed near Grindon while flying in relief supplies during the great freeze-up of 1947, when Grindon was cut off for several weeks by snow.

The stone pillar by the church gate is a rindle stone, bearing the inscription 'The Lord of the Manor of Grindon established his right to this Rindle at Stafford Assizes on March 17, 1862'. A rindle is a brook which flows only in wet weather – a common feature in these parts. Ossoms Hill (see Walk 27) has a number of fenced-off lead-mine shafts.

Manifold Valley Light Railway

See Walk 26.

Waterhouses

The village is noted mainly as the southern terminus of the Manifold Valley Light Railway, where it met the standard gauge line to Cheadle and Leek. Close by the village are the remains of old lead, copper and iron mines.

The Route

Leave the car park in Grindon by turning left and passing a pond on your left. This is newly created under a Village Improvement Scheme supported by the Peak District National Park, Staffordshire County Council, the Staffordshire Moorlands District Council and British Telecom.

At the first junction, after 50 yards, turn right and at the second, after a mere 10 yards, go left with a small green on your right to a third junction within 30 yards. Turn left again so the Cavalier Inn is on your right. By the far end of the pub, where the road signed to 'The Manifold and Wetton' bends to the left, continue directly ahead into a minor road with a cul-de-sac sign.

After only 20 yards, and by a facing bungalow, fork left into a walled lane, the walls soon giving way to hedgerows. At the first T-junction turn right, pass a wooden footpath post after 50 yards, and continue along the lane in the same direction. Crows and magpies may fly overhead, with blackbird, robin and chaffinch betraying their presence on both sides.

Beyond a stone barn on the left there is a breathtaking view of the Hamps

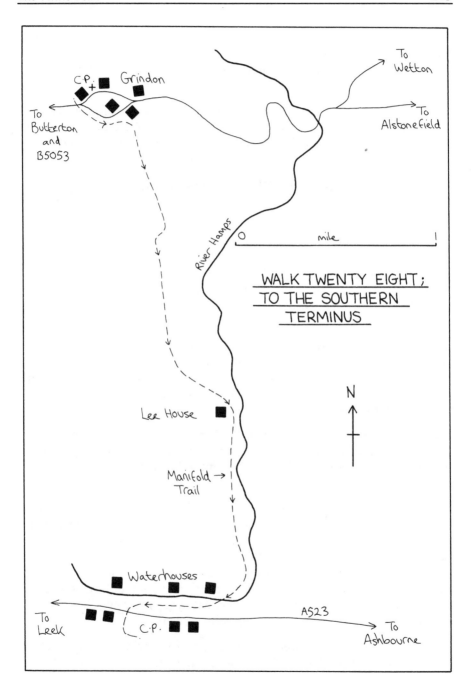

To Wetton

To Alstonefield

C.P. Grindon

To Butterton and B5053

River Hamps

0   mile   1

WALK TWENTY EIGHT;
TO THE SOUTHERN
TERMINUS

N

Lee House

Manifold Trail

Waterhouses

To Leek

C.P.

A523

To Ashbourne

Valley looking towards Alstonefield and Stanshope (see Walk 23). The landscape is patterned by a mixture of hedgerows and drystone walls. The laneside hedges provide a wonderful mix of hawthorn, elder, rowan and wild rose. Slightly to the left is the derelict shell of a former farmhouse.

So far the going has been level with Grindon church steeple directly behind. However, there follows a slight climb to offer a view of Wetton, Narrowdale and the hills around Ecton. This certainly is one of the finest areas not only of the White Peak, but of the Peak District National Park as a whole.

Eventually the lane reaches what can only be described as an apology for a five-barred gate, with a jumble of stones alongside ostensibly forming a stile. There the lane ends.

Continue immediately to the left of a wall while losing height down a field to a stone step stile. Stay forward, still to the left of the wall, while dropping into a side valley of the Hamps. The long, steepish descent passes between two wall corners and, bending sharply to the right, continues downhill even more steeply to a concrete-lined pond.

Keep the pond on your right to reach a stone step stile in the wall on your left. Over this turn leftwards again along a wide track, climbing for a short distance while staying to the right of a wall. Make a bee-line for the stone house ahead. Pass to the left of a group of outbuildings towards a wooden five-barred gate and walk by the front of this rather attractive dwelling to a metal five-barred gate.

There is another pond on your left as the track levels, and you maintain direction roughly parallel with the Hamps Valley which is to your left although the river is not visible at this point. When I came this way in late summer there was, incredibly, a large field of sunflowers at their best.

Beyond another five-barred gate the lane pursues its course straight ahead, but now with a metalled surface. 150 yards beyond the gate, where the lane bends round to the right and by a footpath sign, pass through a small wicket gate. Proceed between a wall on your left and a row of trees on your right. Where the wall corners away to the left, keep forward to a second small wooden gate. Without changing direction descend another large field, by keeping to the right of a stone barn, to negotiate a gap in a row of hawthorns to another small gate with a stone step stile adjacent.

Following the same line descend the next field to a small wooden gate, also with a stile alongside but distinguished by the presence of a holly tree.

Beyond, continue to the right of a row of trees and a fence to a small wooden gate, this time accompanied by a wooden stile. After a further 10 yards turn left through another wicket gate which is partially obscured by hawthorn.

Head diagonally left down the slope towards a notice fastened to the last in a row of dead trees before veering right to pass a barn. Notice the bracket fungus on those dead trees. Stay along the contour following the clear path but, on reaching more trees, this time alive and well, swing right as shown by a crude blue arrow. On a rough track pass through more trees to a metal five-barred gate and then lose height to a wooden one. Veer left to a wooden kissing gate which allows entry onto the Manifold Trail by Lee House. Turn right with the course of the River Hamps on your left.

The river bed is often dry and lined with butterbur but the bent stems show clearly the directional flow of the water. The slopes on either side are covered with trees, and squirrels will often cross your path.

The Manifold Trail crosses a couple of metal bridges as it heads southwards, so the River Hamps is sometimes to the right of you and sometimes to the left. Eventually industry rears its ugly head in the form of the tall chimney of Cauldon Low Quarry coming into view in the distance ahead.

One hundred yards after passing Brown End Farm with its cycle hire business you will reach the A523. Turn right along the pavement. Twenty yards beyond a very distinctive milepost – a relic of the turnpike days – informing you that you are eight miles from Leek, turn left by a footpath finger post to cross the busy major road into a lane. Proceed under an arched stone bridge, continue to the side of a five-barred gate for 100 yards and turn left through another wooden gate. Within yards turn left again for the final few yards to the picnic area and car park. Notice the stone obelisk erected by the parishioners of Waterhouses to mark the Silver Jubilee in 1977. The car park was formerly the goods area for the Manifold Valley Light Railway where it met the main line to Cheadle and Leek.

29. Through Musden Wood

Using mainly paths and tracks, this walk incorporates some of the finest views of the southern extremity of the National Park.

Route: Calton – Musden Wood – Rushley Bridge – River Lodge – Paradise Walk – Ilam Hall.

Start: Calton church. Map reference 104502. Altitude 278 metres.

Finish: National Trust car park, Ilam Hall. Map reference 132506. Altitude 147 metres.

Distance: 3½ miles.

Duration: 2 hours.

Map: The Peak District: White Peak Area, number 24 in the Ordnance Survey Outdoor Leisure series.

Public Transport: Calton has buses from Ilam and Leek on Wednesdays and from Leek and Ashbourne on Saturdays. The village is one mile from the A523 Leek–Ashbourne road which is served by frequent daily buses from Manchester, Stockport, Macclesfield, Leek, Ashbourne and Derby.

Ilam has a bus from Leek on Wednesdays and from Ashbourne on Thursdays and Saturdays. On summer Sundays and Bank Holidays there are buses from Mansfield, Alfreton, Derby and Ashbourne.

By Car: Calton is signed from the A523 a short distance east of Waterhouses. Roadside parking only; please park considerately.

Ilam is reached by minor roads (signed) from the A515 at Tissington Gates and also from the A523 at Calton Moor. National Trust car park at Ilam Hall.

Refreshments: The Manifold café at Ilam Hall serves light meals and snacks.

Along the Way

Calton

The name is Old English for 'Farm of the Calves' which gives us some idea that the agricultural economy in and around Calton has not changed radically for many centuries. Even the pattern of the drystone walls, as at Chelmorton, tends to preserve the old strip system of farming.

The parish church of St Mary is only about 150 years old but is notable for having two clocks: one on the square tower with gold lettering, and a smaller one with black fingers and numerals on the exterior of the south wall. The tower also boasts a magnificent weather cock and there is a sundial in the churchyard.

Parish church, Calton

Musden Woods

These originally formed part of the lands of Musden Grange, owned by the Benedictine monks of Burton Abbey who grazed enormous flocks of sheep in the area.

Ilam

See Walk 25.

The Route

From the church, walk along the village street in an easterly direction, admiring several of the sturdy stone houses as you do so, especially Glebe Farm. Just beyond the farm, which is on your right, make a left turn along a signed footpath which runs between the houses for 100 yards to emerge onto a minor road by Rose Cottage.

Turn right. Pass to the right of an electricity sub-station. 200 yards beyond, just round a bend in the road and by a footpath sign, turn left over a stile alongside a five-barred gate.

Stay close in to the right-hand boundary wall which rises out of an earth bank until reaching a squeezer stile, then walk to the left of a wall to a wooden stile. Continue forward, losing height, along the bottom of a shallow valley with three field boundaries on your left of large hawthorns and rowans – a noticeable change from the customary drystone walls of the Peak District.

Pass a solitary gatepost before meeting a collapsing stone wall on your right. The descent is gradual, with the greensward in summer peppered with purple orchids and purple-headed thistles. There are also plenty of scurrying rabbits and grey squirrels to catch the walker's eye.

Over the next wooden stile, distinguished by a yellow waymark, enter Musden Woods where the path is clear if a little muddy after wet weather. Over another stile there is a fence on your right with the remains of an obvious drystone wall now encrusted with moss. In summer the flora embrace viper's bugloss, red campion and hogweed. The descent continues gradually through the broad-leaved woodland with wood pigeons, jays, rooks and green woodpeckers announcing their presence, along with the diminutive wren. Stand still for a while to catch the secretive rustlings of tiny creatures and a real 'wildwood' atmosphere.

Beyond the next stile the path emerges into a linear glade, enclosed with steep flanking sides, before passing a limestone outcrop on the left by a pair of wooden gateposts. One hundred yards after these go through a large metal gate by some sheep pens to a stile only 50 yards away. A further 20 yards brings you to a footpath sign and the approach road to Musden Grange.

Turn left along the road through the outbuildings of Rushley Farm before dropping down to Rushley Bridge spanning the Manifold. Continue along

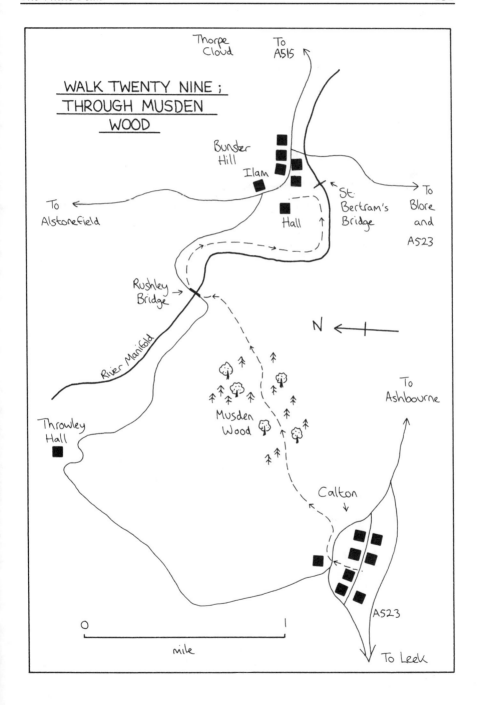

WALK TWENTY NINE ;
THROUGH MUSDEN
WOOD

the road for a quarter of a mile and then turn right through metal gates by River Lodge. Please do remember to put your penny into the collection box. With the oft-dried Manifold to your right, negotiate two stiles in quick succession – both with 'doggy gates', before reaching a metal squeezer stile. Eschew a metal footbridge to your right to enjoy the delights of 'Paradise Walk', a name surviving from the Victorian period when the grounds of Ilam Hall were planned and laid out by the Watts-Russell family.

There are several notable landmarks along the next section, including a Saxon cross known as 'The Battle Stone' – so named because it is said to have been discovered close to the site where the Saxons fought the Danes; the 'Boil Holes' where the Manifold reappears after several miles underground, and Congreve's 'study'.

Remain along the wide path until St Bertram's Bridge. There turn left for the few remaining few yards to the car park at Ilam Hall.

30. By Blore

Mainly following field paths, this route encompasses all that is best in the White Peak.

Route: Swinscoe – Blore – Blore Pastures – Ilam.

Start: The Dog and Partridge Hotel, Swinscoe. Map reference 135481. Altitude 300 metres.

Finish: National Trust car park, Ilam. Map reference 132506. Altitude 147 metres.

Distance: 2½ miles.

Duration: 1½ miles.

Maps: 1. The Peak District: White Peak Area, number 24 in the Ordnance Survey Outdoor Leisure series.

2. Ashbourne and the Churnet Valley, Sheet SK 04/14, number 810 in the Ordnance Survey Pathfinder series.

Public Transport: Swinscoe has a frequent daily bus service from Manchester, Stockport, Macclesfield, Leek, Ashbourne and Derby.

Ilam has a bus from Leek on Wednesdays and from Ashbourne on Thursdays and Saturdays. On summer Sundays and Bank Holidays there are buses from Alfreton, Mansfield, Derby and Ashbourne.

By Car: Swinscoe is on the A523 between Ashbourne and Leek. Park in side roads. Ilam is reached by minor roads (signed) from the A515 at Tissington Gates and also from the A523 at Calton Moor. National Trust car park at Ilam Hall.

Refreshments: The Dog and Partridge Hotel at Swinscoe serves bar meals. Blore Hall has a café, and the Manifold café at Ilam Hall serves light meals and snacks.

Along the Way

Blore

This village, or rather hamlet, half way through our walk, is appropriately named for it means 'windy place', unsurprising considering its exposure on a ridge at 750 feet above sea level. Close by are some Bronze Age burial mounds, only a short distance away from the opening section of our route.

Blore deserved a mention in Domesday Book and references to it in the records of Burton Abbey confirm that it was an outlying grange for the grazing of sheep and deer. The sixteenth-century Hall, now a farmhouse, has been restored; it accommodates visitors and offers afternoon teas and other refreshments.

Apart from the Hall the only other building of any significance is the small church of St Bartholomew with its low, squat tower. This houses three bells, although there is a tradition that originally there were six hanging there; the oldest carries the legend 'God save The Queen, 1590'.

The church itself dates from Norman times but occupies the site of an earlier religious building. The list of clergy goes back to Nicolas of Coventry in 1170. Inside there is a sixteenth-century stone font, seventeenth-century box pews, a fifteenth-century wooden screen and Tudor choir stalls. Elias Ashmole, after whom the Ashmolean Museum in Oxford is named, visited Blore church in 1662 and left an inventory of the medieval stained glass he found there.

Pride of place, however, must go to the magnificent alabaster tomb, erected some time between 1618 and 1640 by Judith, the widow of William Bassett, in memory of her late husband. Later she herself was interred in the vault below. The Bassetts, who arrived from Normandy with the Conqueror in 1066, were an important family in the area, being lords of the manor of Blore for more than 500 years.

It is very rewarding to visit this small church and wander round with the guide leaflet in your hand. Any delay is well worthwhile.

Ilam

See Walk 25.

The Route

Starting opposite the Dog and Partridge Hotel in Swinscoe, walk along the A523 in a westerly direction towards Leek. Only a few yards beyond a wooden bus shelter and a telephone kiosk (on the south side of the road), turn right onto the track leading to Hillend Farm, an impressive stone house set back a little from the main road.

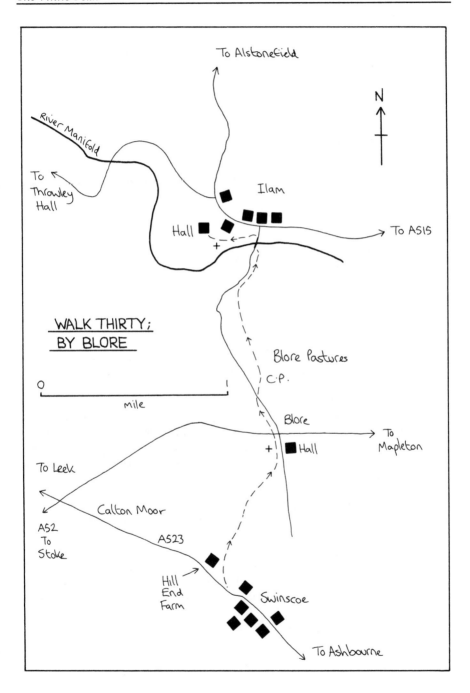

To Alstonefield

N

River Manifold

To Throwley Hall

Ilam

Hall

To A515

WALK THIRTY;
BY BLORE

0   1
        mile

Blore Pastures
C.P.

Blore

Hall

To Mapleton

To Leek

Calton Moor

A52
To Stoke

A523

Hill End Farm

Swinscoe

To Ashbourne

With the farm on your left proceed through a five-barred gate and keep forward to a second. Through that turn sharp left to walk to the right of a wall towards a copse of trees. After 50 yards, however, you will come face to face with a small section of collapsing wall. Turn right so that both the wall and copse are on your left for the duration of a gentle 30-yard climb.

By the far end of the copse negotiate a squeezer stile in a facing wall to experience a view of Bunster Hill and Thorpe Cloud ahead and an extensive panorama of the East Midlands to your right. In the long distance it is just possible to pin-point the tree-crowned summit of Minninglow. Below is the hamlet of Blore with its square-towered church.

Staying close to a wall on your left, lose altitude through two squeezer stiles before veering slightly to the right as the rate of descent quickens appreciably. In the very bottom of the shallow, dry valley, negotiate a stone step-cum-wooden stile before climbing steeply for more than 50 yards, staying to the left of a wall. After the going levels out advance to a wooden five-barred gate in the field corner where a small stone building with a corrugated iron roof stands alongside the gate.

Turn right over a wooden stile, and cross a small paddock to a through stile in wooden fencing. Follow the clear path to the porch of Blore church and continue along the south side to the east end. From there strike out diagonally left to a small wicket gate with a footpath sign adjacent.

Turn left along a minor road, reaching Blore crossroads after 100 yards. Continue straight ahead towards Ilam. On reaching the car park provided by the National Park at Blore Pastures turn right to follow the path through it, losing height gradually to an exit stile at the northern end. Maintain the same line of direction through a second stile on the well-trodden path while descending more rapidly to meet the road just above Oxleisure Farm.

Turn right, cross the cattle grid and continue over the stone bridge. By the memorial in the centre of Ilam village fork left but, where the road to Alstonefield bends round to the right, stay forward for 20 yards before bearing left by a signpost to the church. After 20 yards, and by the entrance to Dovedale House, turn left through a metal kissing gate. Stay to the left of the boundary wall and continue ahead almost to the church. Turn right along the path on the northern side of St Bertram's as it leads to the National Trust car park at Ilam Hall.

We publish a wide range of other titles, including general interest publications, guides to individual towns, and books for outdoor activities centred on walking and cycling in the great outdoors throughout England and Wales. This is a recent selection:

Cycling with Sigma ...

CYCLE UK! The Essential Guide to Leisure Cycling
— Les Lumsdon *(£9.95)*

OFF-BEAT CYCLING & MOUNTAIN BIKING IN THE PEAK DISTRICT
— Clive Smith *(£6.95)*

MORE OFF-BEAT CYCLING IN THE PEAK DISTRICT
— Clive Smith *(£6.95)*

50 BEST CYCLE RIDES IN CHESHIRE
— edited by Graham Beech *(£7.95)*

CYCLING IN THE LAKE DISTRICT
— John Wood *(£7.95)*

CYCLING IN SOUTH WALES
— Rosemary Evans *(£7.95)*

CYCLING IN THE COTSWOLDS
— Stephen Hill *(£7.95)*

BY-WAY BIKING IN THE CHILTERNS
— Henry Tindell *(£7.95)*

Country Walking ...

RAMBLES IN NORTH WALES — Roger Redfern
HERITAGE WALKS IN THE PEAK DISTRICT — Clive Price
EAST CHESHIRE WALKS — Graham Beech
WEST CHESHIRE WALKS — Jen Darling

WEST PENNINE WALKS – Mike Cresswell

STAFFORDSHIRE WALKS – Les Lumsdon

NEWARK AND SHERWOOD RAMBLES – Malcolm McKenzie

NORTH NOTTINGHAMSHIRE RAMBLES – Malcolm McKenzie

RAMBLES AROUND NOTTINGHAM & DERBY – Keith Taylor

RAMBLES AROUND MANCHESTER – Mike Cresswell

WESTERN LAKELAND RAMBLES – Gordon Brown *(£5.95)*

WELSH WALKS: Dolgellau and the Cambrian Coast
– Laurence Main and Morag Perrott *(£5.95)*

WELSH WALKS: Aberystwyth and District
– Laurence Main and Morag Perrott *(£5.95)*

WEST PENNINE WALKS – Mike Cresswell

CHALLENGING WALKS IN NORTH-WEST BRITAIN – Ron Astley *(£9.95)*

WALKING PEAKLAND TRACKWAYS – Mike Cresswell *(£7.95)*

– all of the above books are currently £6.95 each, except where indicated

If you enjoy walking 'on the level', be sure to read:

MOSTLY DOWNHILL, Leisurely Walks in the Lake District

MOSTLY DOWNHILL, Leisurely Walks in the White Peak

MOSTLY DOWNHILL, Leisurely Walks in the Dark Peak

Easy, enjoyable walking books; all £6.95

Long-distance walks:

For long-distance walks enthusiasts, we have several books including:

THE GREATER MANCHESTER BOUNDARY WALK – Graham Phythian

THE THIRLMERE WAY – Tim Cappelli

THE FURNESS TRAIL – Tim Cappelli

THE MARCHES WAY – Les Lumsdon

THE TWO ROSES WAY – Peter Billington, Eric Slater,
Bill Greenwood and Clive Edwards

THE RED ROSE WALK – Tom Schofield

FROM WHARFEDALE TO WESTMORLAND:
Historical walks through the Yorkshire Dales – Aline Watson

THE WEST YORKSHIRE WAY – Nicholas Parrott

– all £6.95 each

The Best Pub Walks!

Sigma publish the widest range of "Pub Walks" guides, covering just about every popular walking destination in England and Wales. Each book includes 25–30 interesting walks and varied suitable for individuals or family groups. *The walks are based on "Real Ale" inns of character and are all accessible by public transport.*

Areas covered include

Cheshire • Dartmoor • Exmoor • Isle of Wight • Yorkshire Dales • Peak District • Lake District • Cotswolds • Mendips • Cornwall • Lancashire • Oxfordshire • Snowdonia • Devon • Northumbria • Snowdonia • Manchester

... and dozens more – all £6.95 each!

General interest:

THE INCREDIBLY BIASED BEER GUIDE – Ruth Herman
This is the most comprehensive guide to Britain's smaller breweries and the pubs where you can sample their products. Produced with the collaboration of the Small Independent Brewers' Association and including a half-price subscription to The Beer Lovers' Club. *£6.95*

DIAL 999 – EMERGENCY SERVICES IN ACTION – John Creighton
Re-live the excitement as fire engines rush to disasters. See dramatic rescues on land and sea. Read how the professionals keep a clear head and swing into action. *£6.95*

THE ALABAMA AFFAIR – David Hollett
This is an account of Britain's rôle in the American Civil War. Read how Merseyside dockyards supplied ships for the Confederate navy, thereby supporting the slave trade. The *Alabama* was the most famous of the 'Laird Rams', and was chased half way across the world before being sunk ignominiously. *£6.95*

PEAK DISTRICT DIARY – Roger Redfern
An evocative book, celebrating the glorious countryside of the Peak District. The book is based on Roger's popular column in *The Guardian* newspaper and is profusely illustrated with stunning photographs. *£6.95*

I REMAIN, YOUR SON JACK – J. C. Morten (edited by Sheila Morten)
A collection of almost 200 letters, as featured on BBC TV, telling the moving story of a young soldier in the First World War. Profusely illustrated with contemporary photographs. *£8.95*